# Body language secrets

Diana Mather

Diana Mather trained as an actress, where she learned that body language and mannerisms are fundamental to building believable characters. Her subsequent career as a BBC television presenter found her reading body language closely in her role as an interviewer. After leaving the BBC in the 1990s, she formed Public Image to provide training in public speaking, media training, international business etiquette, social skills (where body language plays a crucial part) and modern manners to professional and businesspeople. Public Image now has offices in Angola, Kenya, Mauritius and Uganda, as well as working partnerships in Chile, China, Ghana, Nigeria, Russia and Tanzania. Working with people from different cultures requires excellent communication skills, including the ability to decipher the many aspects of body language. She speaks at seminars worldwide and is a regular contributor to British and American media discussions about these skills.

Teach®
Yourself

# Body language
# secrets

Diana Mather

**Also available in ebook**

# Contents

# Acknowledgements

To my very good friend and colleague William Hanson for the use of his image in this book.

To my business partner, Jo Wheeler, for her contribution, help and encouragement.

To Tracey Childs, Margaret Fraser, Joan Gilby, Sue Hardy, Mo Oakden, John Walkley and John Lees for their time and expertise.

To my editor, Hilary Marsden, for her patience and guidance.

Lastly, to my sisters, Ros and Louise, and my children, Leonie and Oliver, for always being there.

The author and publisher would like to thank the following for their permission to reproduce photographs in this book.

Chapter 1 © Scott Griessel – Fotolia; © Nelli Shuyskaya – Fotolia

Chapter 3 © Alexander Raths – Fotolia

Chapter 4 © Bubbles Photolibrary – Alamy; © William Hanson

Chapter 5 © jonasginter – Fotolia

Chapter 6 © Yuri Arcurs – Fotolia; © Andres Rodriguez – Fotolia

Chapter 7 © Rido – Fotolia

Chapter 8 © Monkey Business – Fotolia; © Taylor Jackson – Fotolia

Chapter 10 © wellphoto – Fotolia

Chapter 11 © Bananastock/Photolibrary Group Ltd – Getty Images

Chapter 12 © Piotr Marcinski – Fotolia; © Fotowerk – Fotolia

Chapter 13 © nito – Fotolia; © Tom Wang – Fotolia; © Image Source – Alamy

Chapter 14 © eddie toro – Fotolia

# Introduction

This book is written from a practical rather than an academic point of view and is intended to be helpful whether you are studying body language for business or social purposes. It looks at reading and using body language in a variety of different situations and aims to be a comprehensive guide to making the most of social and corporate occasions.

Body language matters. Understanding the body language of your partner or children can create harmony in personal relationships. Being able to evaluate body language also helps when on a date; the body language of each sex can be quite different and is therefore easily misconstrued. In an employment context, body language can make a significant difference to your chances of getting a job or promotion. The way we stand and walk has a direct influence on how we are perceived, so that all-important first impression is formed as soon as we enter the interview room. Networking is part of business life these days, so being able to read the body language of people you have never met enables you to know how to start a conversation and join a group of people who are ready to welcome you, rather than interrupting an earnest conversation.

I travel frequently and have spent many hours people-watching. It is fascinating to watch couples out for dinner and assess the stage and depth of their relationship! When travelling abroad, knowing the acceptable body language of a country can help you enjoy a holiday or win a lucrative business contract. If you have to appear on the broadcast media, knowing how you come across to a journalist or on camera can help you make the most of interviews.

Getting to know your body is vital if you are to use body language effectively. The way you walk, stand and sit says a lot about you before you have spoken a word, so I will be giving tips and advice to help you make the most of your posture. One thing that is often neglected in body language books is the voice. It is a key part of how we come across to others, having a significant impact on how we are perceived, in particular if our first encounter with someone is over the phone. I have given special attention to this vital part of body language; for me, having trained as an actress, the voice is one of the most powerful tools you possess. This is especially true when public speaking. Many books have been written on that subject, but I have tried to bring together the spoken and visual aspects of body language in this context. It is so very important to use the voice and the body well to make our message hit home – we don't get a second chance to make a positive first impression!

Diana Mather

Cheshire 2012

# 1

# Body language – what is it?

**In this chapter you will learn:**

- ▶ *why body language is important*
- ▶ *how to read non-verbal communication*
- ▶ *what 'inborn actions' are*
- ▶ *what 'absorbed actions' are.*

## Self-assessment

1 What is body language?

2 What are the two things we notice first about others?

3 How do you promote positive body language?

4 Are clothes a part of body language?

5 Why is diet important?

6 What has fitness to do with body language?

7 What are inborn actions?

8 What are absorbed actions?

9 Why is eye contact important?

10 Are most people aware of body language?

Answers are at the end of this chapter.

# Why it is important

Why is body language important? It is important because it encompasses many different things.

► posture

► gestures

► voice

► clothes.

These all go towards creating what is called 'body language', a language that transmits conscious and subconscious signals and messages in your dealings with others that is unique to you. I am sure you are usually aware of the conscious messages you send but often unaware of the unconscious signals you convey. This book will teach your to understand what it is your body is saying and how to transmit those messages in the way you want them to be received. There is no point in stating something vocally if your body is saying something else.

## Key idea

'Always be a first-rate version of you, rather than a second-rate version of someone else.'

Judy Garland

2

Think of your body as your shop window – it has got to be spotless and polished! Seriously, if a shop window looks dusty, lacklustre and out of date it will not attract customers. It is the same with your body.

Clean, healthy skin, shining hair and bright eyes present an appealing picture and therefore help you promote yourself, whether it is in the social or business arena. The better you feel, the more you will be at ease and therefore the more you can control your body language. Positive body language must come from the head and the heart to be sincere, but knowing the negative signals means you can eliminate them. Too much alcohol and not enough sleep has a detrimental effect on body language as tiredness and fatigue means that people tend to yawn, they don't concentrate properly and their posture is poor. A bad diet has a negative effect on your body, as does any sort of addiction; smoking, for example, will show negative body language when another nicotine hit is required. To look good, feel good and make the best of your body you need to eat foods that are going to help replenish cells quickly, give you energy and, more importantly, give you pleasure too. You are what you eat!

**Try it now**

✻  Eat at least three portions of cooked or raw vegetables every day.
✻  If you have to snack, try nuts or dried fruit.
✻  Eat slowly and chew the food properly.

**Remember this**

✻  Fatty meals, fizzy drinks, sweets, biscuits and too much white bread are detrimental to good health.
✻  If you are a 'picker', you can consume a large amount of food without even realizing it.

If you like a drink, it's a good idea to have at least two alcohol-free days a week. Drinking water helps clear the system of toxins, and helps fill a hunger gap between meals. A couple of glasses before a meal can really curb the appetite. A litre a day is the minimum everyone should drink, and still water is better than sparkling.

If drinking plain water doesn't seem particularly appealing, try adding a few slices of lemon, orange or ginger, or a sprig of mint to a jug of water and leaving it in the fridge overnight.

Today, the image of physical fitness and mental alertness is an important one to project, especially at work. The competition to get and keep a job is increasing, and because the trend at the moment is for one employee to 'carry more than one person's workload', to look as though you will be able to stand the strain and cope with the workload is essential! But personal life too is probably just as demanding, as you try to fit more and more into what is for many people an already hectic lifestyle. Too often, lunch breaks slip by with a chocolate bar filling that gap, and a couple of beers or large glasses of wine help to ease the stress of another long day. Not many people are 100 per cent happy with their own bodies, but without necessarily striving for perfection, there are many things you can do to promote a healthy, professional and positive image.

## Remember this

* Drink at least a litre of water a day.
* Cut out junk food and sugary or fizzy drinks.
* Choose fish as an alternative to red meat.
* Eat fewer fatty foods.
* Cut down on tea, coffee, alcohol and dairy products.
* Make sure you eat a balanced diet of protein, carbohydrate and fresh, raw fruit and vegetables.

Looking pasty and unhealthy does not earn praise or promotion, and in this book you will learn some tips on how to ensure your unique body language says what you want it to say. The way you react to other people says a lot. Try to think about the effect your actions and reactions will have on others. Good, positive body language will show that you care not only about yourself, but also about other people. We have to show respect for others, which in turn brings respect for ourselves. However strong your message is, if you can't get it across, it's lost.

Glowing skin shows you are fit and healthy. Deep sleep is essential for the body to renew itself as the cells divide at a much faster rate and a growth hormone is released into the blood stream causing regeneration, so it is necessary to ensure that you get a good night's sleep regularly. Deep breathing is also very important as oxygen is vital to cell renewal. Some people can function on four or five hours' sleep a night and others need nine or ten. Whichever category you fit into listen to your body when it tells you it is tired. Protecting and cleansing is the order of the day so it is advisable to wear a moisturizer with UVA and UVB screens, especially in the summer. Foundation with a sunscreen will also help guard against everyday contamination as well as harmful rays. There will be more on looking after your skin in Chapter 2.

Obesity in the West is an increasing problem. The reason for the increase seems to be lack of exercise as well as the amount of fats consumed. Exercise is often easier in the summer because you will tend to be outdoors more. However, if you don't play much sport, try using a bike instead of the car; take the stairs rather than the elevator. Run up escalators, and if you use the Underground or subway, walk up the stairs sometimes. Walking and swimming are good forms of exercise, but make sure you have proper cushioned shoes if you are going jogging or doing a lot of walking. On the other hand, if you can't bear the thought of jogging for miles and you can't get to a gym, there are exercises you can do at home. Even ten minutes every other day is better than nothing. If you haven't got a fitness plan and you don't have much time, put on your favourite music (it helps keep the rhythm) and try this simple routine.

 **Try it now**

1 Always start by warming up with a stretch. Try to touch the ceiling!
2 Reach as high as you can until you feel your spine lengthen, then hold to the count of 20.
3 Put your hands in the air and then bend down to touch your toes with your knees slightly bent. Do this ten times.
4 Keep your hands on your hips, back straight, and gently swing your body from side to side 20 times.
5 Run on the spot for as long as you feel comfortable.
6 Hold your tummy in at all times.

These are short and sweet, but if you do nothing else try to manage the stretching, as it will pay dividends.

I like to keep fit to music, but choose music that has a steady beat but is not too fast, as it is essential that you are comfortable with the speed of each exercise. If you do want to work out at home rather than join a club, there is a wide variety of fitness tapes and DVDs available, so find the one that works for you. Keeping fit is important as far as positive body language is concerned, and if you are at all worried, go and see your doctor before starting any diet or fitness regime.

**Key idea**

If you keep fit, you feel well. If you feel well, you look good.

So how do you go about getting this first, fundamental part of body language right? People usually make up 90 per cent of their mind about somebody within the first 20 to 30 seconds of meeting them – so you don't have time to waste making sure you are projecting the right image. We are naturally attracted to people similar to ourselves; it's a bit like an animal recognizing friend or foe by the colour of their fur and the smell of their skin. The way someone dresses or speaks, the way they walk, the way they eat – all this body language helps to build a picture of them – good or bad!

The fact that I have included clothing in this book might seem strange, but what you wear and how you wear it has a huge effect on body language. There will be more on this in Chapter 4. A few years ago you could judge someone's job, their background and how much money they made by the way they dressed; today it is not as easy, as people tend to dress much the same unless they are in uniform.

**Key idea**

The first things we notice about others are clothes and hair.

So what influences body language? It stems from early childhood and the different things that happen as we grow up. Some things have a positive effect, such as a supportive family, doing well in school or excelling at sport. But the loss of a parent, abuse, divorce, moving house or changing schools a number of times can all cause us to adopt negative body language. You need to know what your body is saying in order to read non-verbal communication from others if you are to make the most of relationships with fellow human beings, and I will be going into detail about all these aspects in the following chapters. Lack of knowledge can also make you transmit negative body language; being confronted by a complicated layout of knives and forks, for example, can be very intimidating. It's all very well for someone to say 'wait to see which one everybody else uses before you start', but what if you are the guest of honour and everybody is waiting for you? It is not easy to present confident body language if you use the fruit knife when everybody else is using a fish knife. People often show anxious body language when they do not know how to address someone with a title, whether it is a noble or professional one. To have the information at your fingertips, whether you use it or not, will give you the confidence to cope with any situation, however grand.

### Key idea

'Always imitate the behaviour of the winners when you lose.'

George Meredith

# How to read non-verbal communication

Negative signals:

- ► avoiding eye contact
- ► looking round the room
- ► looking at a clock or watch
- ► sneering
- ► mouth rubbing
- ► lip licking or biting

- throat clearing
- head scratching
- twisting the neck
- shrugging shoulders
- sitting very straight
- sprawling in a chair
- shifting about in a chair
- arms folded
- wringing hands
- finger drumming
- crossing and uncrossing legs
- foot tapping.

As you can see, there are a large number of overt negative body language signals and all these show tension and suppressed emotion. This is because you are getting into 'fight, flight or fright' mode: to fight the foe, make a quick getaway or remain rooted to the spot. In social and business situations things are usually not so dire, but the genetic response from our ancestors is still the same. If a person is apprehensive, frightened, nervous, angry or bored they will send out some, or all, of these distress signals.

So let's take a look at these tell-tale signs:

- In the West, if people constantly look away when you are talking to them you are likely to think they are either bored, want to talk to someone else or really do not like you. But in some countries it is not considered polite to keep eye contact for too long. However, if you want to know someone's thoughts and build rapport, eye contact is vital because the eyes really are 'the window to the soul'. If people constantly look away or look over your head when talking to you, it means they are looking for an escape route or looking for someone more interesting to talk to. If they keep glancing at their watch or a clock on the wall, it is obvious that they are either late or want to be somewhere else. Sometimes people are quite unaware of how much their bodies are betraying them, and sometimes these mannerisms become habits because no one tells them otherwise. We will look at how to manage these disconcerting negative signals in greater detail in Chapters 5 and 10.

▶ A sneer is at worst a sign of derision and at best an insincere smile. Either way, if you are the recipient of this sort of body language it is a strong sign that you are not held in very high esteem!

▶ Rubbing the mouth can be an indication that someone is not telling the truth; it is almost as if they are embarrassed by the fact they are telling a lie. It is the same when there is continual licking of the lips.

▶ Throat clearing denotes nervousness and uncertainty, as the saliva in the mouth dries up and the throat goes into a nervous spasm.

▶ Vigorous head scratching usually means that someone is frustrated or annoyed. Pent-up emotion can result in a change in body temperature that can make the scalp feel itchy.

▶ When tension in the body builds up, for whatever reason, it has to come out and manifests itself in different ways in different people. A lot of tension builds up in the neck. The poor neck has enough of a job to do holding up the head, which is one of the heaviest parts of the body, so twisting the neck will help ease any tension, thus it shows you are feeling tense.

▶ Shrugging of the shoulders shows frustration or anxiety as the physiological changes in the body send a message to the muscles, ready for the 'fight or flight' scenario.

▶ Sitting ramrod straight is another sign of apprehension or anger. People waiting for a job interview will usually be highly alert and therefore sit up straight. A businessperson infuriated by someone who is late for an appointment will show disapproval by sitting very straight, as will a school teacher or a boss about to reprimand an errant pupil or employee.

▶ The opposite of the 'broom handle down your back' position is the sprawl or lounge. This usually shows disrespect or contempt, or at the very least a total lack of awareness about what such body language is implying.

▶ Shifting about in the chair means you literally cannot sit still. There can be several reasons for this: excitement, irritation or simply wanting to go to the loo (especially in children!). But in adults it is usually a negative sign exhibiting boredom or impatience.

▶ Anyone who has ever perused a body language book will have read that arms folded across the chest are a barrier position. This stance allows the arms to shield one of the most vulnerable parts of the body. It can be a barrier position but it can also show that someone is cold, shy or just likes standing like that. Whatever the reason, it sends out negative signals because it can imply arrogance, stubbornness, vulnerability or nervousness.

▶ Wringing of the hands shows anxiety and uneasiness. It is as if someone is trying to wash their troubles away.

► Hands can be still or fluttering. Often hands show tension and anxiety by 'washing' or tapping even though face and body may appear calm and in control.

► Finger drumming nearly always denotes irritation.

► Crossing and uncrossing the legs in a man is a negative sign as it shows impatience or exasperation. The body is saying 'what are you waiting for, let's get out of here', and someone who does this either wants to end a meeting or move the conversation onto another subject. A woman, on the other hand, will sometimes use crossing and uncrossing her legs to attract a man's attention, which could be interpreted as a positive signal, or to distract him, which is negative – for him at least!

► Foot tapping, like finger drumming, nearly always denotes annoyance. A client or customer may seem politely attentive when listening to a salesperson, but the tapping foot behind the desk shows that he or she is not interested but impatient to finish the interview and be elsewhere.

Positive signals:

► good eye contact

► smiling

► nodding

► hands clasped loosely on the lap

► sitting or standing in a relaxed position

► leaning forward when listening

► displaying a sense of calm.

Let us look at the positive signs in more detail. These signals make you look confident, trustworthy and in control.

► Good eye contact is vital if you are to build rapport with somebody. You can gauge their inner feelings and encourage them to talk just by 'looking them in the eye'. Staring, however, is not good as it can make you look aggressive and make the other person feel uncomfortable. When you are talking to someone, look away every so often but always meet their gaze after a few seconds.

▶ Smiling is one of the best ways to get people to warm to you. It is a fundamental human signal of warmth and friendliness. However, the smile must be genuine and a full (often known as Duchenne) smile which reaches the eyes, not just the mouth, and it should also come from the heart. It is true that 'putting on a happy face' really does make you feel better, as a smile sends signals to the brain that you are feeling OK.

▶ Nodding also encourages others to talk as it gives them the impression you are interested to know more. Journalists often use nodding and smiling to get interviewees to carry on talking, leading them into saying more than they meant to say!

▶ Hands clasped loosely on the lap show that you are relaxed. When you are nervous and anxious you will tend to clench your fists, getting ready for 'fight or flight', so keeping the hands still shows you are composed and on top of things.

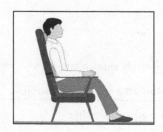

▶ Sitting or standing in a relaxed position has exactly the same effect. People who are apprehensive and ill at ease are usually restless, and this will often show itself by walking around or constantly moving.

▶ Sitting forward when listening shows real interest and concern for the person and what is being said. You also lean forward when you want your listener's full attention or agreement. Either way, it is a very positive signal.

▶ Displaying a sense of stillness and composure shows you are in control of yourself and your situation. It sends out signals of tranquillity and authority, which are also infectious and can help to calm others.

## Key idea

'Wear a smile and have friends; wear a scowl and have wrinkles.'

George Eliot

Today you have the technology to analyse yourself and learn to understand your body language. Strategically placing a video camera when you are on the phone or eating a meal with the family will help you evaluate your body language as well as theirs. It is extremely useful to see how people interact and to make sure children, especially, get their say. Often the quietest sibling will be itching to get a point across but cannot get the parent's attention because the louder, more extrovert brothers or sisters hold the stage. If this goes on for years, these more timid children can grow up to be shy adults with body language that exhibits low self-esteem.

## Try it now

1 Watch your children when you are all having a meal.
2 Notice how much they move in their chair when they want to speak.
3 Give them a chance to say what they want to say.
4 Make sure everyone listens.

# What are inborn actions?

Inborn actions are those that 'come naturally', things you do not have to be taught to do. For instance, babies have the inborn action of suckling as soon as they are put to their mother's breast. Smiling and frowning are common in all cultures and, again, this is not learned or copied behaviour. We know this because blind and deaf babies smile and frown at appropriate times. Deaf babies also cry, even though they have never heard anyone crying. It seems that human brains are preprogrammed to react to certain stimuli without having to learn these actions.

## What are absorbed actions?

Absorbed actions are unconsciously acquired as you grow up, often without you even realizing it. These you learn from those around you. Many family members have the same mannerisms, which they have picked up from their mother or father, or from older siblings.

**Try it now**

Are you right- or left-thumbed?
1 Clasp your hands together and see which thumb is on top.
2 Try and put the other thumb on top.
3 See which is the most comfortable.

Apart from absorbed actions there is 'absorbed behaviour'. For instance, if you have grown up in a family that is very musical or reads a lot, you will be more likely to appreciate music or read a lot too.

**Remember this**

Positive body language often comes from confidence, and there are a number of things you can do to boost your confidence levels.
✳ Meeting new people widens horizons.
✳ Doing new things creates confidence.
✳ Confidence triggers positive body language.

Expanding your horizons and increasing your overall education help to enable you to feel at home in different environments. The more relaxed you are the more your body will be in accord with your brain, thus transmitting positive body language. So anything you can do to add to your knowledge base will help you to gain both confidence and positive body language.

## Key idea

'Everybody lives and acts partly according to his own, partly according to other people's ideas.'

Leo Tolstoy

## Answers to the self-assessment

1 The conscious and subconscious signals our bodies send to each other

2 Clothes and hair

3 Smiling, making eye contact, being relaxed

4 Yes, they are the first thing we notice about others and they affect the way we use our bodies

5 A good diet gives you energy and makes your body function properly

6 Fit people have more positive body language as fitness affects the way you stand, move and your energy levels

7 Those you are born with

8 The actions you learn from others when you are young

9 It shows trust, openness and friendliness

10 No, most people take what their bodies do for granted. It is a language you should learn if you are to make the most of business and social opportunities.

## Focus points

The main points to remember from this chapter are:

- body language is transmitted at both conscious and unconscious levels
- to create positive body language the mind and body must be in harmony
- it is important to look after your body
- your body is your shop window
- learn to study body language.

## Next step

The next chapter will help you to get to know your body. Unless you know your body you cannot learn to eliminate negative body language signals and promote the positive. It is only by examining the body in detail that you can learn to use body language effectively.

# 2

# Knowing your body

**In this chapter, you will learn about:**

► *your mind*
► *your head*
► *your face*
► *your eyes*
► *your nose*
► *your mouth*
► *your shoulders*
► *your arms*
► *your hands*
► *your legs*
► *your feet.*

Take a long hard look at yourself and try to decide how you come across to the world, and then ask a couple of friends how they see you. It's often a shock to discover how differently the rest of the world perceives the image you think you are projecting! The fact that your body and voice are the tools of your trade, whatever that trade may be, is something that cannot be stressed enough, so self-analysis is something you need to do, however painful it might be!

## Self-assessment

1 Why is good posture important?

2 Why is good eye contact important?

3 How can you improve your knowledge?

4 What do drumming fingers denote?

5 What signals a 'barrier position'?

6 What did Italian ladies use to make their pupils larger?

7 Which arm position can help you concentrate for longer?

8 Which side do you look when you are remembering?

9 Why do people rub their noses when under stress?

10 What does constant blinking denote?

Answers are at the end of this chapter.

# Your mind

Positive body language starts in the mind. The minute your feet hit the floor in the morning an optimistic outlook is essential for positive, vibrant body language. If you are feeling depressed it will show. Negative body language has a way of seeping out of your mind and into your body. This 'seepage' or 'leakage' will show many of the negative signals we discussed in Chapter 1.

Try to think positive thoughts and see the opportunities that life has to offer rather than succumbing to its problems. It is easier said than done, but thinking happy and positive thoughts has a positive effect on your mind and body. Depression and prolonged negative thinking will affect the immune system and leave you more prone to illness. All this shows in the way you use your body and the positive or negative image you project. It is also true that if you behave in a confident manner the brain will begin to believe you are feeling confident, thus making a 'virtuous cycle' between behaving confidently and feeling confident.

### Key idea

'You are the same today as you'll be in five years except for two things: the people you meet and the books you read.'

Charlie 'Tremendous' Jones

So what books, papers and magazines do you read? It's not easy to have a conversation at all levels if you only read the tabloids and *Hello!* magazine. Reading a serious newspaper at least once a week, as well as magazines such as *Time* or *National Geographic* will keep you informed about world opinion and events. Nobody expects you to be a political analyst or an expert on the economy, but if you are among a group of people and cannot contribute sensibly to a discussion, it doesn't do much to enhance self-esteem or confidence!

# The upper body

### YOUR HEAD

Hold your head up! Nothing sends out more submissive body language than a bowed head. In some cases it will be an appropriate posture, for instance, when meeting royalty or senior businesspeople from other cultures perhaps. On the whole, however, keep your chin parallel to the ground, eyes looking straight ahead and stand and walk tall. This not only makes you look confident and in control, it helps you feel that way too!

### YOUR FACE

One of the first things people will notice about you is your face. Scowling, grimacing or frowning are all negative body language, as people usually adopt these expressions when they are angry, perplexed or worried, but a smile immediately gives the impression of warmth and confidence. On the other hand, you might also frown when you are concentrating hard or deeply absorbed in something. When I worked as a television presenter I interviewed people for various programmes, and I was horrified when I watched the playback to see that I was often frowning when listening to their answers. I was listening so intently that I was not aware of the body language I was using. Apart from the fact that I did not look particularly pleasant, I was not getting the best out of the interviewees. When I realized what I was doing I stopped frowning and adopted a more open manner, nodding and smiling to encourage them to talk. This way, I got far more out of the interviews, as people could see I was interested in what they had to say and therefore gave me much more information.

### Key idea

'The world is like a mirror: frown at it and it frowns at you; smile, and it smiles too.'

Viscount Samuel

Facial (and bodily) adornments are also part of some people's body language and some are more permanent than others. Tattoos, piercings and scarring have been adopted for thousands of years but they can send out negative signals and, it should be remembered, are usually irreversible. Make-up has also been used for many centuries. Some of it was heavily scented and some was antiseptic to protect the skin. Face masks made of egg white were used to cover wrinkles, while reddish ochre gave the skin a healthy colour. From Tudor times until the 18th century, lead was used in make-up and this resulted in terrible skin damage and sometimes death. Many bizarre methods were used to try to cover the ravages of toxins and disease, including patches and beauty spots. These developed a language of their own; at the court of Louis XV, wearing a patch at the corner of the eye, for instance, was a sign of passion, while at the centre of the cheek meant merriment and by the nose sauciness!

**Try it now: The two-minute facelift**

1 Using a good moisturizer, put some on your fingertips.
2 Place some above your lips, around the mouth and on your chin.
3 Massage moisturizer into these areas with an upward motion for a count of 20, which should take about 20 seconds.
4 Next, place moisturizer on your cheeks and do the same for 20 seconds.
5 Place a little moisturizer or, if you prefer, eye cream on the sensitive eye area, and massage gently into the 'crows feet' (if you have any!), above, and below the eye for another 20 seconds.
6 Place moisturizer on your forehead and massage for a count of 20.
7 Do the same on your neck, first on the right for 20 seconds and then on the left for 20 seconds.

Skin sends out all kinds of messages. Good skin says you are healthy and good skin looks attractive. In the past, a white face denoted upper class status and privilege because most people worked outdoors and had a ruddy, tanned complexion. During the 20th century the situation was reversed as many people worked in factories or offices, which meant pallid white faces, so a suntan showed you could afford to spend time in the sun or go abroad on holiday. Now too much sun is deemed harmful, a more lightly tanned look is considered sensible.

So looking after your face is another important part of sending out positive body language signals. Cleanse the face thoroughly at night with a lotion, cream or rinse-off gel. After you have cleansed, a toner closes the pores. Follow this with a good night cream. Any of the big stores or beauty salons will be happy to give you advice. Many more men are having treatments these days. Having a facial is not only good for the skin, as it helps circulation, but it is a marvellously relaxing experience and therefore helps you to look and feel tranquil and in control. A massage will not only help relax tense muscles and calm frayed nerves, but will stimulate the blood supply and help release toxins that build up in the body. Afterwards, drink plenty of water to enable your system to flush out as much waste as possible. Even if you are frantically busy, it's worth trying to find an hour in your diary (possibly over lunchtime) as the amount of energy that can be restored by a period of deep relaxation is enormous.

## YOUR EYES

Eyes really are the window to the soul, so make the most of them! I have already mentioned how avoiding or evading eye contact sends out negative signals, so you need to actively encourage a steady gaze. This should not develop into a stare, but good eye contact allows you to build rapport with the person or people to whom you are talking. Human beings tend to look to the right when they are trying to remember or recall something and to the left if they are making something up or lying. There will be more on eye contact in Chapter 10.

## Remember this

* Eye rubbing shows tiredness or uncertainty.
* Glazed eyes show boredom or wandering attention.
* Constant blinking can show insecurity or nervousness.
* Squinting can denote dishonesty.

Blinking a lot is a sign of nervousness, as it implies you are trying to shut out the world around you, like children who shut their eyes if they are frightened or angry. People, especially women, with big eyes are thought to be very appealing, so how can you make the most of your eyes? Eye make-up has been used since at least the time of the ancient Egyptians, when both sexes accentuated these very important features. Cleopatra used black galena on her eyebrows and painted her upper eyelids deep blue and her lower lids bright green. For women, good mascara is essential. Choose one that you like and which applies easily. If your eyes tend to water, waterproof mascara could be just what you need. For paler eyes, especially green or hazel, brown is a softer option than black. If you have grey or blue eyes, a dark navy might make a change. For fair-haired people with very pale lashes, having them dyed is a good option. Eyeshadows are made in every colour of the rainbow now and there are creams, powders and pencils; again, personal preference is what counts. However, avoid colours that detract from the eye's natural hue.

In past centuries, Italian women who wanted to make themselves more attractive squeezed drops of deadly nightshade into their eyes to enlarge the pupils. It is also known as belladonna, or 'beautiful lady'. Flashing eyes can give out differing signals, some of which are of a sexual nature. A man or woman who flashes their eyes a lot is usually trying to appear attractive to the opposite sex, as they are drawing attention to 'the windows to their soul'. There will be more on the body language of dating in Chapter 11.

These days, many men with very pale eyelashes and eyebrows dye them, and it does help to highlight their eyes. Eyebrows need to be tidy for both sexes as very heavy brows can give the impression that you are frowning or feeling grumpy.

## ▶ Glasses

The wrong shape of glasses can spoil an attractive face. However much you may like a particular style, do make sure it suits you before you buy what can be an expensive item. The top of the spectacles should be in line with your eyebrows, and the bottom should be no lower than the top of your cheekbones. If in doubt, ask your optician for advice. Fashion glasses can make a statement and wearing glasses can be used to give an air of authority, but wearing sunglasses can create a barrier, so unless the sun is really bright it is better to take them off so that those you are talking to can see into your eyes. Try not to use glasses as 'props' to chew or fiddle with, as these negative actions will distract people from what you are saying – unless, of course, you want to use this sort of body language to show boredom or disagreement. Make sure glasses fit properly too; squinting or constantly looking over the rim of glasses because they do not fit properly sends negative signals.

## ▶ Eye hygiene

Eyes should be checked regularly, as eye tests can act as an early warning system for a number of ailments, including high blood pressure, as well as catching incipient eye conditions such as glaucoma. If you wear contact lenses, make sure you keep them really clean or they can cause permanent damage to the eyes.

## YOUR NOSE

The man who made rubbing his nose famous was the former US president Bill Clinton, when asked about his relationship during the Monica Lewinsky inquiry. The reason for this? Blood rushes to the surface of the skin in times of stress and noses can become engorged, making them itch or feel uncomfortable. This usually happens when you are trying to avoid answering difficult questions, so the gesture is best avoided. If you feel an itch coming on, get out your handkerchief and blow your nose, unless you are in Japan; there's more on the different meanings of body language in different cultures in Chapter 12.

Flared nostrils are a sign of anger, passion or extreme anxiety, caused by the breath becoming faster owing to emotional pressure from the 'fight or flight' urge.

## YOUR MOUTH

When you stand in front of the mirror what do you see? You have probably been taught that it is vain to spend too much time looking at yourself, and that self-analysis is only for psychology students. Of course, to spend the day contemplating your navel, or anything else for that matter, wouldn't do you or anyone else any good, but it is important to realize your strengths and weaknesses. A winning smile can be a great 'strength'. It not only makes you look welcoming and friendly but it will also warm your voice when you talk, and this is especially important when using the phone. A smile will not only influence how someone reacts to you face to face, but it can physically make you feel better. The act of smiling sends signals to the brain to say that you are feeling happy.

 **Try it now**

1 Smile into a mirror.
2 Give a half smile – how do you feel?
3 Give a full smile that reaches your eyes – how do you feel?
4 Wait for happier thoughts and a feeling of optimism.

A one-sided smile usually means that the person is not really happy or in accord (they do not find your joke very funny, for example) but is trying their best to send out positive signals. A grin, or wide smile, will show your teeth so make sure they are cleaned and flossed regularly. These days it is easy to get teeth whitened if they become yellow, but each treatment removes a little of the enamel so it is important to be aware of what will stain the teeth. Smoking or drinking too much coffee or red wine can all cause staining, so regular visits to the dental hygienist will help to ensure a sparkling smile.

**Key idea**

'A smile is a curve that sets everything straight.'

Phyllis Diller

Covering the mouth or putting your hands to your mouth can indicate that you are not telling the truth or, at best, that you are unsure of what you are saying. Again, it goes back to childhood as children try to stop themselves talking by pressing their hands to their mouths. Biting or licking the lips too much also shows apprehension or unease, as when you are under stress your breath will come in shorter gasps, making the lips dry.

**YOUR HAIR**

Hair projects an immediate image: the 'dumb blonde', the 'fiery redhead' or the 'passionate brunette'. Those images are stereotypes, but your hair can say whether you are healthy or not and how much you care about your appearance. In past times, people wore wigs to make a statement or show their status in society rather than to subtly cover thinning hair. In the 18th century, women wore incredibly intricate wigs that were woven into their own hair and could be up to 30 inches high! They had to have special pillows made so that they could sleep at night, as they would often wear the wigs for at least a week. As you might imagine, these wigs were a breeding ground for bugs and parasites, and women used to have long pins so that they could scratch their itching heads. Men would have their hair cropped or shaved under their wigs and would quite often take off their wigs when in relaxed surroundings to give their heads an airing; unlike Louis XIV of France, who went bald at the age of 32 and had his wig passed to him through the bed curtain before he got up and passed it out after getting into bed so that nobody would ever see the royal pate. I am not sure what happened when he was with his wife! Men's wigs were also part of their body language and were worn to show status. The 'Macaroni' wig was so high it took at least three heads of hair to make, and the term 'bigwig' was coined to mean somebody who was rich and important.

Your hair should be your crowning glory, but a poor diet, smoking, medication and too many late nights all have a detrimental effect on hair. So how can you keep your hair in peak condition? A good diet is fundamental, followed by a good haircut, as it will show your face to the best advantage. When you have found somebody you trust, who listens to what you say and cuts your hair in a style that suits you, stay with them! A good haircut should last six to eight weeks before it starts to look out of shape. If you are working in an office or have a senior position, long hair can undermine credibility unless it is put up or tied back; this applies to men and women alike.

**Remember this**

- Eat a well-balanced diet.
- Choose a hairstyle that suits your type of hair.
- Have a good cut.
- Keep hair tied back in the office.

I will also mention facial hair here. Men once prized beards as a mark of both masculinity and sexuality. Now, however, there is a prejudice against beards and stubble seems to suffice as a masculine signal. For a job interview I advise men to be clean-shaven (unless there are religious reasons for having a beard); as you do not know what views your interviewer might have on facial hair, it is better to be safe than sorry.

### YOUR SHOULDERS

Shrugging the shoulders is a negative gesture because it sends out a message of 'don't know', 'cannot be bothered', or even ruder meanings in some countries! Rolling the shoulders shows a build-up of tension, indicating that the person is ill at ease. To send out positive signals, stand tall and keep your shoulders back but relaxed.

## YOUR ARMS

You use your arms to wave, to hug, to push away as well as all the other things you need them for every day. You also use them to gesticulate when making a point. Big open gestures are important when making presentations to a large audience, as long as they are not distracting, but if used in normal conversation such gestures can appear theatrical and insincere. An arms akimbo stance suggests power and dominance. The famous picture of King Henry VIII was meant to show that he was a powerful monarch in control of his realm.

Sometimes crossing one's arms can have a positive effect. If you have a complex problem to solve, try crossing your arms to solve it. This is what researchers asked participants to do in a research project in 2008. They found that the participants worked roughly twice as long at a set of difficult anagrams and their persistence led to a greater number of correct solutions.

## YOUR HANDS

Hands have a language all of their own and can tell you much about the inner thoughts and feelings of others over and above simply emphasizing a point or helping to 'paint a picture' when telling a story or making a presentation. Some cultures use their hands more than others. It may be something to do with the weather, as people living in warm climates seem to use their hands more than those living in colder climes; they probably keep their hands in their pockets to keep them warm! An even balance between speech and hand gestures adds animation to a conversation and increases interest in the audience.

Wringing or 'washing' the hands usually means anxiety; it is as if you are trying to wash away the problem. I have a friend who would continually twiddle her thumbs during a conversation. It was very distracting because the rest of her body language was calm and attentive. She would smile, nod and show interest in what I was saying as well as responding appropriately, it was the thumbs that made me feel uneasy. Eventually I asked her what was wrong and she told me her husband was having an affair. She had no idea that her hands were betraying her inner anxiety. Now her problems have been resolved and her hands are calm again, reflecting her inner mood.

Twiddling or wringing the hands can also indicate frustration; it can be a sign of wanting to end a conversation or needing to be somewhere else. This is most often seen when meetings overrun, for example. Placing hands on hips can imply stubbornness or vexation. Pointing is considered rude in most cultures because it is seen as a hostile gesture. It is almost like pointing a weapon and is usually used by people when they are angry or want to make a very strong point. It is best avoided, or kept for those occasions when you need to make an aggressive point, as it can send out very negative signals.

Finger tapping or drumming also shows worry or impatience, as does tapping the side of the face or rubbing the back of the neck. Again, the 'fight or flight' mode is brewing inside us and because we are in a situation where we cannot do either of these things, the body language leaks out in whatever way it can.

Fingers in mouths or nail-biting shows insecurity or anxiety. This goes back to early childhood when we suckled at our mother's breast not only for food but also for comfort. A hand constantly fiddling with hair or scratching the head sends out the same sort of signals. Head-scratching can also denote nits or tiredness, as mentioned in Chapter 1. Either way, these are not good signals to be transmitting!

Some people shake their hands as if they are suffering from cramp. This again shows a very high degree of stress and tension which has manifested itself in an uncomfortable stiffening of the wrists.

Hands are a very important part of your body language, so you should keep them in good condition. They should be kept well moisturized and it is a good idea to use suncream every day as soon as the weather gets warm, especially in the car, to prevent sun-induced age spots; this applies to both men and women.

Nails must always be clean, whether they are long or short, and a regular manicure doesn't go amiss. For women, nail polish should never be chipped. I know of a company that lost a big training contract because its representative had chipped nail polish. The competition was so fierce that something that small proved to be the deciding factor. It was not the nails themselves, of course; the fact that the person involved had not taken the time or trouble to reapply her nail polish raised doubts about her commitment to herself and therefore to the demanding project she was competing for.

### Remember this
* Keep nails spotlessly clean.
* Manicure regularly.
* Don't put your hands to your face.
* Think calming thoughts and your hands will be calm.

# The lower body

### LEGS

Crossing and uncrossing the legs can tell different stories. Constantly changing position shows a lack of comfort and concentration. Sometimes it can be because a chair is uncomfortable, or it can indicate that people are tired and desperately trying to keep awake and concentrate. Crossing the legs can show displeasure, too. It is also a ploy used in dating, as is rubbing one calf against another, something discussed in more detail in Chapter 11. Women going barelegged in the summer should make sure legs are waxed and moisturized regularly. Men should also make sure their legs look good if they are going to wear shorts.

Rolling the ankles shows boredom or frustration. All these signals are signs of a pent-up 'fight or flight' mode seeping out of your body subconsciously.

### FEET

Tapping the feet is usually a sign of impatience or anxiety, as is shifting from foot to foot when standing. However, women may do this if their shoes are hurting them; I try to minimize such movements when I am standing teaching for eight hours in my most fashionable, but most uncomfortable shoes!

Feet will often point in the direction of your subconscious thoughts. If you watch people at a party or networking group, feet are a good indicator of how the conversation is going. If two people are talking and the person being 'talked to' is bodily square on but one foot is pointing away, then that person is probably thinking they would rather be somewhere else!

Reflexology is a therapy based on the theory that energy channels, known as zones or meridians, pass through every organ of the body and end in the feet – which contain 72,000 nerve endings. The Chinese have used this treatment for thousands of years and it has become extremely popular worldwide. By massaging specific areas of the feet, reflexologists are able to work on corresponding areas of the body. It can prove beneficial for many complaints, such as backache, PMT, migraine, acne, eczema and psoriasis. Reflexology is a stimulating and revitalizing experience for the whole body, and can be of real benefit, especially at times of stress.

## Answers to self-assessment

1 Because it will make you look confident and will send out positive signals

2 It allows you to build rapport

3 By reading more

4 Impatience and unease

5 Arms folded across the chest

6 Belladonna

7 Folded arms

8 To the right

9 Because blood rushes to the skin's surface and noses can become engorged in times of stress

10 Insecurity or nervousness.

## Focus points

The main points to remember from this chapter are:

✳ a smile makes a good first impression
✳ keep hands and feet still when under pressure
✳ keep as fit as possible
✳ maintain good eye contact
✳ make sure you are aware of the image you are projecting.

## Next step

**In Chapter 3 you are going to concentrate on your voice, your second most important communication tool, especially as the telephone is often the first contact you will have with prospective clients or employees. Knowing your voice is essential if you are going to communicate well, and I will be helping you to make the most of that potentially wonderful instrument.**

# 3

# The voice

In this chapter you will learn:

▶ *how to make the most of your voice*
▶ *how to speak clearly*
▶ *vowels and consonants*
▶ *vocal exercises*
▶ *how to listen properly*
▶ *how to use the phone effectively.*

## Self-assessment

1 How do you make sure that you speak clearly?

2 How do you strengthen your voice?

3 What makes a voice interesting?

4 What should you do to be a good listener?

5 Why is correct breathing essential to good voice production?

6 What are the Three Ps?

7 Why are tongue-twisters helpful?

8 Which consonants are the most important?

9 When should your phone be switched off?

10 Name three things you should know about your voice.

# How to make the most of your voice

The voice is a wonderful instrument but most people have no idea how they sound, as very few bother to listen to their voices. Whether you are chatting with family and friends at home, colleagues at work, giving a talk or making a speech, using your voice well is vital.

What is a good voice? The voice is like an instrument which, when properly played, will enable you to connect with and fascinate your audience. If you want to play an instrument well you have to get to know it and then you have to practise. It is exactly the same with the voice. We are fortunate enough today to have recording devices that enable us to hear exactly how we sound, so you have no excuse not to make the most of your voice. Some people are born with better voices than others, with a bigger vocal range and a warmer or richer tone, but that does not mean that you can't make the most of the voice you have. I cannot stress enough the importance of listening to yourself. It is only by knowing your voice that you can learn to use it to your advantage – this means that you know:

▶ how fast you speak

▶ how clearly you speak

▶ whether your voice sounds interesting.

A pause can be central to people taking on board what you are saying as well as helping you control the audience, as it can help emphasize a point, while silence is a great way to make people realize that they are the only ones talking! If, however, the pause is too long, it can sound as though you have forgotten what you were saying.

## Key idea

Few people have any idea how they sound and those that do, do not like the sound of their own voices, so listen and learn!

'It is not what you say, but the way that you say it' that makes people remember you and take notice. The way you use your voice is vital if you want to make a confident impression, and good diction is fundamental to being easily understood. Accents can cause bias, especially if they are very strong; but they shouldn't be a problem unless they are difficult for anyone from outside that region to understand. Unless you feel that you are at a disadvantage from betraying your origins, don't try to lose an accent. If, however, you feel uncertain because of it, there are exercises and tuition available to help you speak more clearly and eloquently. The most important thing is to be understood wherever you are, and that means speaking clearly and audibly – and with plenty of preparation if you are doing it in public. There will be more on making presentations in Chapter 7.

## Try it now

1 Record yourself chatting with your family or friends.
2 Listen to the recording.
3 Analyse how you sound.

It makes a huge difference to your overall body language if you use your voice and body in accord, and I cannot stress enough that this can only be done by listening to your voice and experimenting with the Three Ps:

▶ pace
▶ pitch
▶ pause.

## PACE

Pace is very important if you want to be easily understood. Speaking at a pace that people can keep up with will keep them interested. Most people speak much faster than they realize, which means that some listeners will switch off or only pick up one word in three. It is just as bad to speak too slowly, as your listeners will switch off because they are bored. So again, recording a few sentences from a newspaper, book or magazine will enable you to get to know your natural pace and discover whether it is too fast or too slow. If you think you are speaking too fast, listening to your voice regularly will enable you to feel when you are rushing, so you can consciously take a breath and slow down. If you realize you are droning on and speaking too slowly, try reading something a little faster, record it and listen back. You must feel comfortable with the pace at which you speak, and practice does make perfect!

## PITCH

Pitch is probably the most vital of the Three Ps as the rise and fall of your voice makes any conversation or presentation more interesting and enjoyable. The pitch of your voice will determine how the message is received. Male voices tend to have a lower register than most female voices. If the pitch of a female voice is very high it can lack credibility in the workplace, especially for a public figure. The former British prime minister Margaret Thatcher lowered the pitch of her voice, especially for Prime Minister's Questions in the House of Commons, at the suggestion of her advisers as they felt it gave her more authority. This was true, as women's pitch tends to rise when under duress or when they are angry.

It is important to change the pitch of your voice during a conversation or a presentation rather than keeping it on one level. If you find you speak in a monotone, then practise raising and lowering your voice to change the pitch and listen to how you sound.

So if you want to change and vary the pitch you need to start listening to and analysing your voice.

## Try it now

1 Read this sentence in different pitches: 'I want to make this point as I feel it is important.'
2 Try it in a higher register than you normally use.
3 Try it in a lower register than you normally use.
4 Try it in your normal voice.
5 Now record the sentences in the different styles and analyse the results. Which sounds more effective?

### PAUSE

As I have mentioned, a pause not only enables your listeners to keep up with what you are saying, it can also emphasize a point and help you gain attention. If you pause after a significant fact, for example, people will take more notice of it than if you just carry on to the next point. If others are talking when you are trying to speak, there is nothing like silence to make them realize that they are the only ones talking!

## Remember this

* Pace is the rate at which you speak.
* Pitch is where you place your voice.
* Pause when you need to emphasize a point or gain attention.

## Key idea

You have to get to know your voice in order to be able to use it well.

# How to speak clearly

One of the most crucial factors in producing clear speech is to open your mouth – many people would do well in auditions to become a ventriloquist! If you don't open your mouth wide enough, your words cannot come out clearly and your diction will be poor.

## Try it now

1 Stand in front of a mirror.
2 Say 'How Now Brown Cow'.
3 Say it again opening your mouth wider.
See and hear the difference.

Breathing correctly is also vital for good voice control.

## Try it now

1 Breathe in and say the months of the year as you expel the breath.
2 Try humming and filling the resonators in your head so that you can feel your head throbbing.
3 Read a poem or a passage of prose and mark the places where you need to breathe.
4 Whisper the piece, then gradually increase the volume.
5 Be aware of your lips, mouth and tongue.
6 Practise saying words in an exaggerated way so that you can feel your tongue, lips and mouth moving.

This is another exercise. Say each line and build up your breath control.

I

I must

I must control my

I must control my breath

I must control my breath and

I must control my breath and sustain

I must control my breath and sustain my

I must control my breath and sustain my sentences

## Remember this

✻ Breathing correctly is essential for good voice control and production.
✻ It is important to practise breathing exercises to develop your control of these muscles.

✻ Controlling the muscles helps to produce your voice at varying volumes, with longer phrasing and ease of speech.

Breathing correctly for speech means following this sequence.

✻ As you breathe in, push your ribcage outwards and upwards, increasing the size of the chest.

✻ The diaphragm (a dome-shaped muscle across the ribcage) descends and the chest increases and more breath fills the lungs.

✻ The diaphragm rises again while the ribs stay in the same position and air is expelled.

✻ The ribs descend and further air is expelled.

Sound is caused by the breath striking the vocal cords and it is best to try and be as relaxed as possible. Tensing causes the breath to be shorter and the voice poor. Place your fingertips together on your diaphragm, take a deep breath and expand the ribcage outwards and upwards to increase the size of the chest. Your fingers should come apart as you breathe in and meet again as you breathe out.

**Try it now**

1 Breathe in again (keeping your fingertips where they are) and hold the breath for a count of 5 before breathing out.

2 Breathe in to a count of 5, then hum as you expel the air.

3 Keep your mouth closed so that you can hear the sound resonate in your head as you expel the air.

4 Next, breathe in to a count of 5, then say 'aah' as you expel the air with your mouth open.

Continue the exercises until you have increased your breath control so you are able to hum and say 'aah' comfortably up to a count of 10.

Try these exercises again but making the humming softer, then louder. Do the same with the 'aahs'. These exercises help increase your breath control, which is vital for clear speech.

# Vowels and consonants

A, E, I, O and U make up the vowel sounds in English. They should be pronounced ai, ee, eye, oh, you. In English there are both regional and international variations depending on where you live, but using 'received pronunciation' will enable you to be understood easily throughout the world.

The most important consonants are T and D. Consonants are essential because they help punctuate speech and slow it down. If speech is too fast and indistinct it is difficult to understand. The overuse of headphones and earpieces may mean that a growing number of people will experience hearing loss in their thirties and forties, so clear pronunciation will become even more critical. In words like 'get', 'it', 'and', etc, the T or D needs to be pronounced clearly to make speech easily understood.

# Vocal exercises

Record your voice as you read the lines bringing out the true meanings of the words, i.e. make the cake sound delicious or disgusting!

It's a lovely cake.

It's a delicious cake.

It's a gorgeous cake.

It's a dry cake.

It's a stale cake.

It's a disgusting cake.

Where you place the stress can subtly alter the meaning of what you are saying, so it is important to put the stress on the words that carry the most weight, that is, the words that will point the listener to the exact meaning of the sentence.

Record these sentences and only stress the words in capitals.

HOW many guests were there?

How MANY guests were there?

How many GUESTS were there?

How many guests WERE there?

How many guests were THERE?

You should be able to hear the difference in the questions; it is subtle but important.

Tongue-twisters are like taking your mouth to the gym. Repeat each phrase about three times, beginning softly and increasing the volume through the second and third repeats. Keep the words clear and sharp, paying special attention to the consonants. All these exercises work on limbering up the muscles we use for articulation. They also make you read what you see and not what you think you see, therefore keeping the brain and mouth in gear, and will enable you to achieve clear speech if practised regularly.

▶ Twist the twine tightly round the three tree trunks.

▶ Did Dora dare to deceive David deliberately?

▶ Kate Cooney carefully closed the kitchen cupboards.

▶ Gregory Gartside gained good gradings in Greek grammar.

▶ Naughty Nora has no nice neighbours.

▶ Little Larry Lester lolled lazily on the lilo.

▶ Peggy Babcock, Babcock Peggy.

▶ Red leather, yellow leather, red lorry, yellow lorry.

▶ Unique New York, New York unique.

▶ Fresh fried fish.

▶ A cracked cricket critic.

▶ The seething sea ceaseth and thus sufficeth us.

▶ She sells seashells on the seashore. The shells she sells, sell for sure.

▶ Sister Susie sews shirts for sailors.

▶ Round the rugged rocks the ragged rascals ran.

▶ Theophilus Thistle, the successful thistle-sifter, in sifting a sieve full of unsifted thistles, thrust three thousand thistles through the thick of his thumb.

- How much wood could a woodchuck chuck, if a woodchuck could chuck wood? As much good wood as a woodchuck could chuck, if a woodchuck could chuck wood.

- Peter Piper picked a peck of pickled peppers. If Peter Piper picked a peck of pickled peppers, where's the peck of pickled peppers Peter Piper picked?

- Betty Botter bought some butter. But said she my butter's bitter. If I put it in my batter it will make my batter bitter. So she bought some better butter and it made her batter better.

- Swan swam over the sea. Swim swan swim. Swan swam back again. Well swum swan.

 **Try it now**

Take a deep breath before each sentence and say:
1 I can make my voice rise higher and higher and higher.
2 I can make my voice go deeper and deeper and deeper.
Use the upper and lower register of your voice.

# How to listen properly

To listen to somebody properly you have to look at them. Not only do you lip read much more than you are aware of, but you need to see their faces to read the body language that goes with the voice. If you say to someone 'How are you?' and are texting or looking away when they reply 'Fine, thank you', you cannot tell whether they really are fine unless you are looking at them. The voice could be cheerful because they want you to think everything is OK, but there could be a sadness in their eyes that tells you this is not the case. Many misunderstandings between life partners and friends – never mind work colleagues or clients – happen because people have not listened with care and attention.

If you are trying to understand a tricky problem or a complicated scenario, repeat the main points to make sure you have understood correctly. Listen for changes in voices you know well and look into people's eyes when you listen to them as well as speak with them. Eye contact is vital in reading body language.

## How to use the phone effectively

Research shows that smiling when using the phone helps to warm the voice; give it a try and I think you will agree. Speak a little more slowly than normal and make sure you enunciate clearly, especially on mobile phones as you can never be sure how good the reception is.

Try to concentrate as much as possible. I know I am guilty of emptying the dishwasher or feeding the dog while chatting on the phone. This is fine if the call is just a chat, but if the call concerns something important, give it your full attention; you wouldn't be doing other things if the other person was in the room with you.

When having a serious conversation on the phone, you need to be able to concentrate to read the other person's voice as you can't see their face or body language. If it is a business call, clear your desk so that you can concentrate fully, and make sure you have a pen and paper handy so you can take notes; it is easy to forget minor points in a conversation that later turn out to be highly significant.

If you have a voicemail message on your home or work phone or your mobile, make sure you sound cheerful, warm and welcoming. It might be the first time the caller hears your voice, so use the techniques described in this book to create a good first impression.

However, there are two situations when the phone should always be switched off:

► in meetings – research is being carried out to work out how much time and money is wasted at business meetings all over the world by people using their mobile phones. This is not only disrespectful and extreme bad manners, but it wastes productive time and therefore money because it often means a meeting will start late, run late and be less effective than it should be. Unless there is a good reason, phones should be turned off or at least put on silent during a meeting with anyone. If you are trying to sell a concept, product or service to someone and are constantly stopping to answer the phone, you are very likely to lose your train of thought (never mind your client or customer) and therefore vital opportunities can be missed if you don't give the meeting your full attention.

► at mealtimes – always switch off the phone or put it on silent when dining with others, and don't leave it on the table or you will be drawn to it like a magnet. Socially, going out for a meal should be an enjoyable event, but if someone is constantly answering the phone it spoils the occasion for everyone. There was a time when it was unusual and therefore somewhat thrilling when your date suddenly answered the phone during dinner, but those days are long past and now a romantic dinner for two can suddenly become a rather unromantic threesome if the mobile joins you at the table. Much business is done over the breakfast, lunch and dinner table, so if you are constantly answering the phone you are implying that the person you are with is not as important as anyone else who happens to call. Many deals have been lost because of this sort of crass behaviour. The people you are with at the time should take priority over everyone else. If you have to leave your phone on for a really important call, tell the assembled company and then make the conversation as brief and unobtrusive as possible when it rings. Leave the table if it is going to take time and suggest that the others continue eating. If you are dining with just one person, be as quick as possible, otherwise they don't know whether to carry on, let their food get cold or just go home!

It is the height of bad manners to text while you are talking to someone. It is impossible to have two conversations at once and give them both equal consideration. If you have to text, excuse yourself and don't start the conversation until you have finished. However, the text is hardly ever so important that it has to be answered immediately! You owe it to the person you are in conversation with to give them your full attention, so ignore the phone until you have finished chatting.

## Remember this

- Don't use the phone during meetings.
- Don't use the phone when eating with others.
- Don't text while in conversation with others.

## Answers to self-assessment

1. By opening your mouth and using good diction
2. By doing vocal exercises and breathing techniques
3. Using the Eight Ps
4. Maintain eye contact and nod your head in agreement
5. Because it helps you produce a strong, clear voice
6. Pace, pitch and pause
7. Because they limber up the mouth
8. T and D
9. At mealtimes and in meetings
10. How fast you speak, how clearly you speak, and whether your voice sounds interesting.

## Focus points

The main points to remember from this chapter are:

* get to know your voice
* record yourself regularly
* practise breathing correctly
* it's not just what you say but the way you say it
* learn to love your voice!

## Next step

In Chapter 4 we will look at deportment. The way you sit, stand and walk says a lot about you, and I will be giving you tips on looking and feeling confident, in control, elegant and sophisticated.

# 4

# Body language in deportment

**In this chapter you will learn:**

- ▶ *how to make a positive first impression*
- ▶ *how to stand with self-assurance*
- ▶ *how to sit with composure*
- ▶ *how to walk with confidence and poise*
- ▶ *how to enter and leave a room with style*
- ▶ *the elegant way to climb stairs*
- ▶ *the graceful way to get in and out of a car*
- ▶ *what your clothes say about you.*

## Self-assessment

1 Why should you stand up straight?

2 How should women get into a car gracefully?

3 What helps disguise short legs?

4 Why is it essential to smile?

5 Where should you place hands when seated?

6 What makes 'a good walk'?

7 Why is walking with a book on your head good for deportment?

8 Name three typical body shapes.

9 Why is image important?

10 What is good deportment when sitting?

Answers are at the end of this chapter.

# How to make a positive first impression

Making a positive first impression is vital – you don't get a second chance to make a one. And the single most important tool in making a positive first impression is a smile! A smile immediately sends out signals of friendliness and welcome, and I make no apologies for mentioning this again.

## Key idea

The last thing you should put on before you leave the house is your smile!

Deportment comes from the Latin word *deportare*, meaning 'to carry', so deportment is how you carry yourself. This means that the way you stand, sit and walk all contribute to that all-important positive impression. So many people wear trainers and jeans at home or to travel to and from work, even if they change when they get to the office, that there's a tendency to walk in a sloppy, and sometimes ungainly, way. What does this say about you? If you stand badly it gives an impression of a lack of drive or ambition. If you slouch in a chair, it gives the impression you are not really paying attention. If you drag your feet, it can give the impression of laziness or muscle weakness. Such traits point to a lack of caring about yourself. Of course, all these impressions may be entirely misplaced, but can you take that chance? In a job interview or a meeting with customers or clients, I don't think you can leave anything to chance. The actress and theatre producer Tracey Childs went to ballet school when she was young and says: 'This helped enormously with my deportment as our posture was very important. Walking tall when going on stage or entering a room made you feel, as well as look, confident; something that has helped me all my life.'

## Remember this

* Good deportment is important as it affects the way you breathe and the way you speak.
* Good posture is essential if you are to feel and portray confidence.

# How to stand with self-assurance

Standing is part of everyday life so make sure you look good and feel comfortable. Keeping your spine 'in line', i.e. 'standing up straight', is essential to maintaining good posture and good health as well as projecting positive body language.

### Key idea

If you want to feel more powerful, adopt a powerful posture. Researchers reported in 2010 that when people stood or sat for one minute in powerful poses – those involving open limbs and expansive gestures – they not only felt more powerful but also had increased levels of testosterone in their system. When you dominate the space, your mind gets the message.

Good shoes are crucial if your lifestyle entails a lot of standing because pain and discomfort show on your face. Fashion may have to go by the board if your job requires you to stand most of the day. Comfortable shoes usually cost more, but they are worth it. Make sure they are always kept in good condition and put shoetrees or paper in them when you are not wearing them. Black shoes go with most outfits, or cream, for women, in the summer. As a man, if you have large feet, don't wear very pointed shoes, as they will look even larger. A slight heel for women is deemed more professional in the office than very high heels or flat shoes.

### Try it now

1 Stand tall with your head up. The fact that you are looking people in the eye will help you achieve parity with them.
2 Roll your shoulders round up to your ears and then down until they rest naturally.
3 Pull your stomach in.
4 Tighten your buttocks.
5 Let your arms hang by your sides, keeping them behind the side-seams of your clothes. This helps keep your shoulders back.

# How to sit with composure

Most people have no idea how they look when they sit, and yet you sit in front of others daily, so your body language should portray the image you want to project. Before sitting down, feel the chair with the back of the legs, then lower yourself onto the seat and rest your 'bottom' at the back of the chair. This allows you to sit straight but feel comfortable. If you are small, sit in the middle of the chair, keeping your back straight, as dangling legs do not give confident body signals! At girls' boarding schools up to the 1950s, the 'young ladies' were made to sit with a rod down the back of their dresses to make them sit up 'ramrod' straight! While this is excessive, sitting slumped like a sack of potatoes gives out extremely negative signs.

Hands should rest one on top of the other or clasped in the lap. Legs or ankles can be crossed, but for women, knees and ankles should always be together to look elegant. The 'ankle on knee' look for men is not a good one, nor is splayed legs; you may be inordinately proud of your 'crown jewels' but there is a time and a place! Before standing up, move slightly to the front of the chair and rise in a fluid movement without pushing heavily with your hands or flapping your elbows.

# How to move with confidence and poise

At my company we make all our students practise walking with a book on their heads! It is a throwback to Victorian times when young ladies were taught the basics of deportment in this way, but it is just as relevant today. It makes you keep your head straight and helps you walk elegantly, whether you are a man or a woman. A good walk really does make a difference to your body language.

### Remember this

* Head down when walking shows a lack of confidence
* Nose in the air suggests arrogance
* A straight back when walking portrays confidence
* A slight smile shows confidence, warmth and friendliness.

### Key idea

You should not take huge steps or look as if you are hurrying. You should walk with eyes looking straight ahead and chin parallel to the ground – this will give an air of confidence and competence as well as keeping your spine in line.

Jo Wheeler, a weather presenter on Sky News who was a model before she became a radio and television presenter, believes the importance of deportment 'is evenly divided between what it does for the individual and how they are seen by others. Bad deportment and a slovenly shuffle is a bit like trying to drive a car with a flat tyre and a twisted chassis. The long-term effect will be to exert stresses and strains on parts of the body that weren't designed for it. Bad backs, stiff necks, shoulder tension and flabby midriffs will follow. Any sportsman or woman will know that when the body is working as it should, it has the fluidity and grace of a well-built machine.'

'In terms of projecting an image, there is nothing as easy as walking well and sitting properly. It makes you look self-assured (happy in your own skin) and confident in who and what you are. The head needs to be up, the shoulders back, and the upper body near stationary whilst all the walking motion moves subtly through the feet, ankles, knees and hips. Think of skiing where the knees bear the brunt of the undulations underfoot.'

## Try it now

1 Place one foot in front of the other as you walk.
2 Your weight should be transferred slowly from heel to toe.
3 Full body weight is not transferred until the foot is flat down.
4 This pulls the hips forward and the body should follow gracefully.

The result is a casual yet defined style of walking that looks as good in the office as it does on the catwalk (where it is very exaggerated). In practice, this feels slow, and slightly ridiculous, but it's amazing how quickly it becomes second nature.

## Try it now

1 Take confident strides – neither too long nor too short.
2 Keep your shoulders still and arms relaxed.
3 Keep your chin parallel to the ground.
4 Keep your eyes looking straight ahead.

## ENTERING AND LEAVING A ROOM WITH STYLE

When entering a room, look at the people you are meeting, close the door behind you without looking at it and *smile*! You should be able to gain their full attention immediately.

When leaving, keep looking at the people you are saying goodbye to, open and close the door without showing your back so that the last thing they see is your smiling face.

## THE GRACEFUL WAY TO CLIMB STAIRS

When climbing stairs it is as well to keep a hand on the banister in case you should trip. Place the feet at a slight angle, towards the banister. This means that the entire foot will fit comfortably on the step, and the direction of your foot placement will throw you towards the safety of the banister should you slip. Allow one hand to glide up the banister at your hip level and look straight ahead. Try not to grab the banister and heave yourself up the stairs!

When descending the stairs, let the hand move smoothly down the banister and remember to keep your head up at all times! Again, angle the feet towards the banister to avoid a headlong fall.

## THE ELEGANT WAY TO GET IN AND OUT OF A CAR

This applies more to women than men (unless they are wearing a kilt). When getting into a car wearing a dress or skirt, sit on the seat first and then swing the legs in, keeping knees and ankles together. When alighting, swing the legs out first, knees together, and push up with the hands to enable you to stand.

# What your clothes say about you

Image plays a highly significant part in today's culture – in both business and social life. It is influential because so much of the way you judge and are judged is visual, and how you look makes an enormous impact. What you see shouldn't just be what you get, it must make the other person want to find out more.

## Key idea

'Fashion can be bought. Style one must possess.'

Edna Woolman Chase

As I have said, the first thing people notice about others are their clothes. The way you dress says so much about you. Most humans have worn some sort of clothing since the species started to walk on two legs. As they moved away from the warm climes of Africa, it also became necessary to wear clothes to keep warm. In the past it was easy to see who was who and what they did by the clothes they wore; it was as much part of their body language as speech or gestures. You can still see that in some professions today – soldiers, police officers, nurses, priests to name but a few – but only when they are actually working and in uniform do you know what they do.

## Key idea

'Know, first, who you are; and then adorn yourself accordingly.'

Epictetus

In the reign of Edward IV it was much easier to gauge people's social status because it was actually against the law to dress like a nobleman if you didn't have a title. 'No knight under the rank of a lord ... shall wear any gown, jacket, or cloak, that is not long enough, when he stands upright, to cover his privities and his buttocks, under the penalty of twenty shillings ... No knight under the rank of a lord ... shall wear any shoes or boots having pikes or point, exceeding the length of two inches, under the forfeiture of forty pence ...'. So think how lucky we are today!

### BODY SHAPE

Carolyn Kenmore, a supermodel in the 1970s, famously said, 'You have to have the kind of body that doesn't need a girdle in order to get to pose in one'. Unfortunately, that doesn't apply to most of us and while we long for the 'perfect' shape – long legs, a small waist, firm bust, flat tummy, tight thighs, toned bum, good 'six pack', and so on, but how many people actually measure up to the 'perfect beings' in magazines? Exercise can do a great deal to get your body closer to this ideal, as I have said in Chapter 1, but however hard you try you cannot suddenly grow 30 centimetres, lengthen your legs or shorten your arms. What you can do is to make the most of what you have. We are all different, but without going into too much detail, here are some quick guidelines for the standard male and female shapes for office wear. What you wear at home is obviously important too, but we cannot go into this in detail here. If you want advice on your wardrobe and accessories, a good stylist can give you the advice you need. If you don't know of any, many high street stores have personal shoppers, there are companies listed on the internet, or you could ask a friend.

### ▶ Long-waisted, shorter legs and pear shapes

For women, short jackets are the style to adopt. Try to have belts the same colour as your skirt or trousers, as they help to add length to the lower half of the body. Trousers, leggings and jeans should always come up to the waist, as hipsters make legs look shorter. It is best not to wear your skirts either very short or very long, as this will emphasize the lack of leg length. If you have a small waist, make the most of it by wearing waisted outfits accompanied by a striking belt. If you are slightly pear-shaped, buy a jacket that is loose fitting rather than fitted, as this will help balance your smaller top half. If you are a size bigger on the hips, try adding a waistcoat to a suit to help pad the jacket out, or wear a scarf to keep the attention above the waistline. Avoid very wide skirts and trousers, and choose patterns that are vertical.

For men with this body shape, shorter jackets are also best. Don't wear baggy or wide trousers and make sure your trousers come up to your waist, as hipsters make legs look even shorter. Braces can be fun and will keep the trousers sharp. Trousers should rest on the front of your shoe and finish at the base of the shoe at the back, where it joins the heel - this remains the case whatever the length of your leg. Some men are also pear-shaped, so make sure you have good padding in the shoulders of your jacket to give a balanced look.

### ▶ Short-waisted with long legs

Women will find longer jackets are more flattering, as they hide the fact that there is not much length in the waist. Short, straight skirts and trousers are flattering too, with a belt that is the same colour as your top, as this will add length to your torso. Trouser suits look great, as they show off your length of leg.

Men's jackets should generally be as long as your arms. By this, I mean that if you keep your arms straight and 'cup' your hands, the hem of the jacket should comfortably rest in the cupped palm of your hand. This will make you look in proportion.

### ▶ Triangular shapes

The shape of women has changed a lot over the past 40 years, and we are now seeing women who are taller and triangular-shaped, i.e. with broader shoulders and narrower hips. Make the most of your slim hips and longer legs with straight skirts, either short or long. Pleated skirts look good too, when they are in fashion. Jackets should be tailored, but make sure shoulder pads are not too big as you already have wide shoulders. Dresses will hang well on you, but avoid the belted type, as they will draw attention to your lack of waist.

This shape is a typical male one, but don't over-emphasize your shoulders by wearing very wide jackets with padded shoulders. If you have wide shoulders but shorter legs, don't wear long jackets.

### ▶ Larger people

Women should keep clothes simple and choose good fabrics. Don't wear anything that is too tight. Skirts must not pull and buttons should not strain. Loose, flowing, plain-coloured clothes are most flattering. Long, unstructured jackets or shirts, waistcoats and tunic tops look great. Choose good, striking accessories like a scarf or a brightly printed shawl draped over one shoulder. An eye-catching necklace or brooch also looks very attractive.

It is important for men to make sure clothes fit really well, even if this means getting them made or altered to suit your body shape. The temptation is to buy things smaller than you need, but jackets or sweaters that are too tight don't do you any favours!

## Remember this

✳ Most people have different images for home and work.
✳ The right image takes time and thought.

You need to ask yourself:

✳ Who am I?
✳ What do I do?
✳ What type of image do I want to project?

If you are working, then your image has to be in keeping with the image of your company or organization in order for you to send out positive body language signals. If your job means spending time with the chief executive officer of an international bank, for example, they will probably not be happy if you turned up in jeans and trainers, whereas the chief executive of a trendy advertising company probably would. It all comes down to what is appropriate and what you feel comfortable with. If your employment means you are forced to project an image that doesn't suit you, then you are probably in the wrong job!

## Answers to self-assessment

1 To maintain good posture and good health and project positive body language

2 Sit first, then swing legs into the car, keeping knees and ankles together

3 A Wearing a short jacket elongates legs

4 Because it transmits warmth and friendship

5 On your lap

6 Keeping the head up, shoulders back, upper body nearly stationary, with all the walking motion in the legs and hips, chin parallel to the ground and looking straight ahead

7 Because it helps keep your head up and your back straight

8 Long-waisted, shorter legs and pear shapes; short-waisted with long legs; triangular shapes, larger people

9 Image is important because it defines who and what you are

10 Looking alert and sitting up straight.

## Focus points

The main points to remember from this chapter are:

* ✳ clothes are probably the first things we notice about others
* ✳ keep your clothes in good condition
* ✳ get to know your body shape
* ✳ think about how you walk
* ✳ standing tall makes you look confident

## Next step

**Your next step is to conquer the world of social and business networking. I will be taking you through the dos and don'ts as well as the whys and wherefores of getting your body language right in order to make the most of social and business opportunities.**

# 5

# Social and business networking

In this chapter you will learn:

- ▶ *the art of networking*
- ▶ *the first impression*
- ▶ *meeting and greeting*
- ▶ *reading the crowd*
- ▶ *joining and leaving a group politely*
- ▶ *when to move on.*

**Self-assessment**

1 How should you offer your hand for a handshake?

2 How do you remember people's names?

3 What is the correct greeting?

4 Why is networking important?

5 Where should you look to gauge someone's attention?

6 What should you do if anyone is on their own?

7 Why is reading body language crucial?

8 Name the different 'groups'.

9 Why should you keep your hands out of your pockets?

10 What is a good handshake?

Answers are at the end of this chapter.

# The art of networking

Networking is important because it allows you to advertise yourself and your occupation at minimum cost, so it is an excellent way to build your business. People do business with people they like and trust, so if you are an electrician and prospective customers can see that you look professional and hear that you are competent, they are more likely to both use and recommend you. This goes for any service from banking to hairdressing. Socially, building a network of friends enhances your life.

It is vital to have confident body language when networking for business. We all wonder whether we have the right to expect success. You have every right to success – but you will need to work to achieve it, and one of the ways to achieve success is by networking. Self-confidence is also essential if you are to make new friends.

It is fundamental to look forward to the networking event and see it as an opportunity, so visualize success beforehand. Actually, visualizing success is helpful in any situation, even a confrontation with your boss, partner or children. If, say, you anticipate a problem with your annual appraisal, then you are likely to have one. If you think you will lose an argument with your partner, you more than likely will. If you expect to have a problem getting your children off to school, you will! It is the same with networking events. If you think nobody will want to talk to you they probably won't, because your body language will be negative and drive them away. A positive focus to your life is contagious as it leads to open and positive body language that will draw people towards you. Have the confidence to follow your own judgement about the people you meet. Both positivity and negativity are communicable and pass from person to person. Try to be as supportive as possible to others at these events and they will be supportive of you, which will increase your self-confidence and promote positive body language.

### Try it now

Think of the event you are going to.
1  See yourself entering the room.
2  Visualize yourself talking to people.
3  Visualize exchanging business cards.

Consider how much you have already achieved These achievements can be in any field, either domestic or at work. I can't stress enough that everybody has abilities and accomplishments to be proud of. Analyse yours and focus and concentrate on them. Once you feel confident, plan your strategy. The idea of networking is to meet as many people as possible, especially as far as work is concerned. Somebody once described it as arranging to have a cup of coffee rather than trying to do business at the time.

### Try it now

1  Take out your business card holder.
2  Check the number of cards.
3  Replenish!

# The first impression

In Chapter 1, I mentioned that people usually make up 90 per cent of their mind about somebody within the first 20 to 30 seconds of meeting them. Bearing this in mind, it is crucial you make the right impression immediately at networking events. If you know that you are wearing the 'right' clothes and that you look good, you will feel confident whether it is a social or professional occasion. And *smile* – this does more to make a positive first impression than any other type of body language. It projects the same message in all countries and cultures and can be recognized from at least 30 metres.

Some books tell you that a man with his hand in his pocket looks casual but confident. It certainly looks casual, but if you are hiding something, you are not comfortable; hiding one or both of your hands says you are not quite as confident as you would like to appear – so if in doubt, leave it out! Walk into the room ready to shake hands, smile and show you are looking forward to meeting the people there.

# Meeting and greeting

The correct greeting when you meet someone is still 'How do you do' or 'Good morning', 'Good afternoon' etc; 'Hi' or 'Hiya' is not professional. In my opinion, shaking hands is a vital part of assessing someone's body language as you can tell so much from a handshake.

### Key idea

Shaking hands was a mark of faith and confidence in Roman times.

If it was good enough for the Romans, it is good enough for me! Seriously, it is almost always the only skin-on-skin contact you will have with your customer, client or new friend and it will tell you a lot.

### HANDSHAKES

A handshake is a gesture of friendship and trust. In days gone by men shook hands with the left hand as this was where they habitually kept a dagger concealed up their sleeve; so offering the left hand showed they were not armed. Later it changed to the right hand, as for most men the right arm was usually the 'sword arm'. Leaving the sword in its scabbard and offering his right hand showed that a man did not want to fight. This did not apply to women as they did not shake hands in those days.

The way you offer your hand is important. The whole arm should be extended as you move forward to greet someone, not just the hand.

**Try it now**

1  Stand in front of a mirror.
2  Extend your right hand, keeping your elbow locked to your side.
3  Now extend the whole arm.
4  See which looks more confident.
5  Try it again with a smile!

A firm handshake in a man or a woman usually denotes a confident person with a strong personality, although many women tend to have slightly weaker handshakes. This is especially true in some cultures, but a good firm handshake should be cultivated by everyone in the business world. A dominant person who likes to take control will offer you their hand with the palm facing down. When this happens, take the hand and turn it to the vertical position as you shake it.

If someone is submissive they will offer you their hand with the palm facing up. This is not positive body language as it can give the impression that you are a pushover.

Unless it is for cultural reasons, a weak handshake in a man is always worrying! Nobody likes to be offered a 'wet fish', from either a man or a woman! Anyone in business should be confident enough to give a firm hand, and if you find this difficult or uncomfortable, practise shaking hands with everyone you meet until you develop a handshake that is both confident and comfortable for you. This should show that you are not afraid to take and squeeze the hand of someone you want to do business or be friends with. It must be firm, but not bone-crushingly so.

Some people suffer from wet or clammy hands, if so keep a tissue or handkerchief in your pocket and surreptitiously wipe your hand before you enter a room where you know you are going to be greeting others. Wiping hands with a few drops of cologne can also help to close the pores that allow the hands to become damp. The sweat glands in the palm of the hands are usually activated by anxiety, so a positive attitude to meeting new people can have a beneficial effect.

### Remember this

* A handshake should be equal for both parties.
* Both people's hands should be vertical.
* It should last no longer than five seconds.
* There should be no more than three 'pumps'.

### Key idea

People judge you on a warm, firm handshake.

# Reading the crowd

When you first walk into a room, stand for a moment and smile. This not only makes you look like a warm, friendly and confident human being, it also gives you a chance to sum up the people there. You will automatically analyse how they are dressed, their ages and how like or unlike you they are; this will help you decide who you should approach.

Don't try to enter a 'closed' group. These are people who are facing each other and maintaining eye contact, with their feet pointing towards each other. They will be having some sort of discussion and don't want to be interrupted. An 'open' group will literally have a space that will admit you. People will be standing at a 45 degree angle to each other with one foot pointing slightly away from one another, which shows they are ready to welcome another into their midst.

### PROJECT YOURSELF

Voice and body language play a major part in projecting confidence; the importance of the voice was covered in Chapter 3. To recap, good diction is essential otherwise people will have difficulty in understanding what you are saying, which can lead to unnecessary misunderstandings and poor communication. An obvious tremor in the voice shows nervousness and can sow seeds of doubt as to the validity of what you are saying. An indistinct or monotonous tone will almost certainly turn people off.

Again, the advice on positive body language given in Chapters 2 and 4 holds good here; stand tall, hold your head up and smile as you walk into the room. You are there to be seen so fill that space!

# Joining and leaving a group politely

As long as you read the body language correctly you should find you are welcomed into a new group, so don't hover around like a butterfly trying to find the right flower. Put on your best smile and walk boldly up to the bunch of people you think look the most interesting. Phrases like 'I hope I am not interrupting ...' or 'May I join you ...' before giving your name helps to smooth the path. If it is a business occasion, you would also give your company name and say what you do. You may shake hands at this point, although if people are holding food or a drinks, a nod of the head when smiling to say hello is more appropriate as you don't want them struggling to change hands and find where to put their glass, etc. Again, it is a good idea to repeat someone's name when you respond, for instance 'How do you do, Lucy' or ' Hello, Lucy', to cement it in your mind. At networking meetings people usually have name tags so you don't have to remember names.

I am often asked how to get away from people without causing offence. As I said at the beginning of this chapter, the idea of networking is to meet as many people as possible, so working the room is what is expected. Even socially, it is nice to see as many friends as you can as well as meeting new people, so don't feel obliged to stay with anyone when you have run out of things to say. Expressions such as 'I have really enjoyed talking to you but I mustn't keep you ...' gives others the hint that you want to move on and allows them to get away too. Or 'It has been so nice to meet you, but I must try to see Julia before she leaves. I'll see you later ...' even if you won't, will do the trick.

It is not good manners to leave anyone on their own, so introduce a loner to a new group before moving on. It is also important to watch out for bystanders and strangers. If you see anyone lingering and looking unsure, excuse yourself from those you are with and go and introduce yourself, then present them to the other people. Once they are settled and you have finished your conversation, then you can move on.

### Remember this

* Don't interrupt people mid-conversation.
* Engage bystanders and those on their own.
* Introduce people to each other.
* Ask questions without being too personal or intrusive.
* Don't get stuck with one person or group for too long.
* Politely move on when appropriate.

#### WHEN TO MOVE ON

The time to move on is dictated either by body language or when you have nothing more to say. If someone you are talking to gets a bit restless or begins to lose eye contact, glance fleetingly at their feet to see where they are pointing. If they are pointing away from you, it is a sure sign they are feeling trapped. Saying something like 'I am sure there must be lots of people you want to see, so here is my card and let's make contact next week' allows you to take the upper hand in a business situation as well as showing you are a considerate and well-mannered individual. If conversation becomes half-hearted and you are racking your brain for something to say, it is definitely time to make your excuses and move on!

## Remember this

- Smile as you walk into the room!
- We make up 90 per cent of our minds about people in 20 seconds.
- Dress to impress.
- You are the image of your organization.
- Don't try to enter a 'closed' group.
- Read body language.

## Answers to self-assessment

1 Extend the whole arm, not just the hand
2 By repeating them
3 'How do you do' or 'Good morning/afternoon' etc
4 To build your business
5 Their feet
6 Introduce yourself and then introduce them to others
7 So that you don't overstay your welcome
8 Open and closed
9 To show confidence
10 Warm and firm.

## Focus points

The main points to remember from this chapter are:

* ✳ mix with as many people as you can
* ✳ don't try to do much business at a networking event, just make contacts
* ✳ arrange meetings to discuss business matters further
* ✳ be focused about what you want to achieve
* ✳ take plenty of business cards!

## Next step

If you are employed, you will have to attend meetings as they are a part of business life. Even if you aren't working, most people have sat on a committee of some sort, whether that of a charity, a sports club or the PTA. Meetings are essential to communicate ideas and information, but they can also be a waste of time if they are not necessary or well run. Chapter 6 looks at body language in meetings as well as giving tips on now to make meetings as interesting and productive as possible.

# 6

# Body language in meetings

**In this chapter you will learn:**

- ▶ *where to sit or stand*
- ▶ *how to sit*
- ▶ *how to interject and make your point*
- ▶ *how to show approval or disapproval*
- ▶ *phone, video and Skype conferencing.*

## Self-assessment

**1** How should you sit at a meeting?

**2** How do you interject politely?

**3** Why should you smile on the phone?

**4** What should you do when chairing a conference call?

**5** How do you show approval?

**6** What is the role of the chairperson?

**7** Why is it important to wear work attire for a video or Skype call?

**8** Which way do most people usually look when they are creating thoughts?

**9** Where should you sit in a one-to-one meeting?

**10** What does 'steepling' the fingers denote?

Answers are at the end of the chapter.

Meetings are a fact of life in the corporate world. But many people I have spoken to in my work say that at least 50 per cent of the meetings they attend are badly organized and don't achieve their objectives. Badly managed meetings waste time and can have a negative effect on company morale and teamwork.

Managing meetings is an art; the aim is to get the most out of the meeting in the least amount of time. Whether they are with staff, colleagues or clients, meetings should be:

▶ well-organized

▶ informative

▶ productive.

Time is an important asset in business. If meetings are unproductive or too long, attendees start to resent the time they take, and the company's bottom-line will suffer as time is money.

The role of chairperson is vital as it is his or her responsibility to control the meeting. If you take on that role, you must ensure that only the relevant people are asked to attend and that everything is organized in advance. Notes or minutes should be distributed as soon as possible after the meeting. The chairperson must also insist that questions and comments 'go through the chair' in order to keep the meeting disciplined and to time. If everyone starts embarking on their own agenda, chaos will reign! Reading body language is essential to make sure everybody is given equal time to air their views. If important topics are brought up that are not on the meeting's agenda, fix a time to talk about them or arrange another meeting if the situation is urgent. If possible, avoid introducing an extra matter as it will make everything and everybody run late. As with most things in life, preparation is vital and is the key to successful meetings.

### Remember this

* Appoint a chairperson
* Write an agenda
* Circulate the agenda in advance of the meeting
* Start meetings on time
* Set a time for the meeting to end
* Be realistic – don't try to fit in too much
* Allow everyone to have their say
* Organize visual aids and handouts if needed
* Be strict about time
* Take notes or minutes
* Circulate notes or minutes soon after the meeting has taken place.

Weekly meetings help to keep staff abreast of different projects as well as the state of the company or organization on a regular basis. A weekly agenda can highlight both positive and negative events in a manageable time frame. If you don't need to have meetings weekly, then once or twice a month should suffice. Most people dislike last-minute meetings as it disrupts their routine, so only call one if it is really necessary and give attendees as much warning as possible.

### Key idea

Don't have meetings unless there is something important to discuss.

**Remember this**

✳ Be on time
✳ Keep things short and to the point
✳ Don't wait for latecomers
✳ Keep records
✳ Recap minutes of the previous meeting at the start of the next meeting
✳ Stay focused on the reason for the meeting.

# Where to sit or stand

Where you sit or stand in a meeting can have an influential effect on your particular outcome. It is important to bear in mind how people receive information. For most people the emotional side of our nature is handled by the right hemisphere of the brain and the more logical side by the left hemisphere, but the data is received the other way round! If you stand or sit to the *left* of your 'audience', you will be talking to their right brain, which is good if the subject is more abstract. For facts and figures, it is best to target the left side of the brain, so you would make your presentation standing or sitting to the *right* of your audience.

Tests have shown that people who sit at the front usually learn and retain more than those sitting at either the back or the sides of a room. So if you are running an event, a horseshoe arrangement of the seats is the best layout in order to engage everybody. You can tell when most people are trying to remember something as they will glance to the right. When creating thoughts, or telling untruths, they are more likely to look to the left. Some left-handed people do the opposite so, as with all body language, you have to put things in context.

**Try it now**

✳ Recall an event from last year
✳ Picture the moon on a cloudy night
✳ Imagine you are about to choose from a menu
✳ Think of the last time you went to the cinema.
Remember which side were you looking when recalling the above.

In a one-to-one meeting, try to sit at a 45 degree angle to the other person rather than directly opposite, which can be confrontational, and try not to sit with your back to an open door or space as it can make you feel vulnerable.

## How to sit

It is important to look alert; sitting up straight and leaning slightly forward shows you are interested and listening intently. If, however, you feel somebody is taking too long to make a point, leaning back in your chair and looking at your notes should give the speaker a signal that you have lost interest in what he or she is saying.

Your hands are important whether you are sitting or standing. 'Steepling' the fingers (putting the forefingers or all the fingers together rather like a church steeple) can show concentration and empathy when listening. If someone steeples their hands and you are in rapport, you will do it too. Try to avoid crossing your arms in a barrier position, and keep your hands out of your pockets.

 **Try it now**

1 Place a chair in front of a full-length mirror.
2 Practise sitting up straight.
3 Put your hands in the steeple position.
4 Find a comfortable standing position.

The way you sit is critical if you are to come across well.

# How to interject and make your point

Sometimes you may have to interject to make a point if the chairperson does not ensure that everybody has their say. After all, you are only attending the meeting because you have a contribution to make, so make sure you make it! You might say something like 'I really must come in here as I feel we are going off at a tangent ...'. If it is a formal meeting, you should preface your interjection with 'Mr/Madam chairperson'.

An alternative might be 'May I add something at this point ...', which is a polite but effective way to interject. Lean forwards towards the group as you are speaking and then lean back again when you have finished. When chairing a meeting, check to see who is leaning in, as it is usually a sign they want to say something.

# How to show approval or disapproval

It is very important to praise people when something is done well. Their body language will show you how much praise helps to improve their self-esteem. Nodding your head, smiling and verbally agreeing are ways of showing approval for good ideas and strategies.

On the other hand, shaking your head or even 'tut-tutting' will show others that you disagree with what they are suggesting. If this goes unheeded, then you have to interject. An interjection along the lines of 'I must disagree/strongly disagree with what has just been said ...' (depending on how strongly you disapprove), and then briefly stating why, should allow you to have your say. Do not lose your temper! Losing your temper will also lose you the argument and your credibility. If you feel you are getting heated, use the deep breathing techniques in Chapter 7.

**Try it now**

❋ Stand or sit up straight.
❋ Take a deep breath in for a count of three.
❋ Hold the breath for a count of three.
❋ Exhale for a count of three.
❋ Feel yourself calming down.

# Phone, video and Skype conferencing

I mentioned in Chapter 3, but would like to emphasize again, how smiling when using the phone helps to warm the voice. For a conference call it is also crucial to clear your desk so there are no distractions and your mind is free to listen to the nuances of what is being said. Telephone conference calls should be short and to the point, especially if they are meant to motivate or communicate regular corporate messages. If there are a number of people on the call, you cannot be sure if someone isn't contributing because they have nothing to add or whether they are no longer present! When chairing a call, make sure you talk to everyone involved and ask individuals regular questions; it keeps them alert and attentive.

For video and Skype calls, how you look and what you wear is significant (see also Chapter 9). Make sure you wear something that projects the image you want to project. Even if you are working from home, do not appear in leisure clothes. It is also critical to choose the location carefully, as your surroundings will be visible. If you are always immaculate in the office and your desk is usually tidy it will come as a shock to colleagues or customers to see you in a messy kitchen with debris or children's toys strewn about the place!

Make sure you don't move about too much. Skype can still be unreliable at times, and over-the-top gestures and erratic body language is distracting over a video link. It is also important to ensure you look into the camera, as you want to establish eye contact with the person or people at the other end of the link. And remember at all times that you are the image of your company or organization!

## Answers to self-assessment

1 Upright, but relaxed

2 By leaning forward and saying what you want to say

3 It warms the voice

4 Talk to each individual

5 By nodding and smiling

6 To organize and control the meeting

7 Because you are the image of your company or organization

8 To the left

9 At 45 degrees to the other person

10 Concentration and empathy.

## Focus points

The main points to remember from this chapter are:

* make sure meetings are really necessary
* have an agenda and stick to it
* prepare properly for conference calls
* smile when using the phone
* be prepared to make your point.

## Next step

**Many people have to make a presentation or speak in public at some time in their lives, so learning to enjoy the experience is crucial to doing it well. Chapter 7 takes you through the preparation necessary for speaking in public, to give you confidence and the techniques that will enable you to deliver a speech or presentation with passion and panache!**

# 7

# Body language and public speaking

**In this chapter you will learn:**

- ► *how to prepare your talk*
- ► *how to deliver your talk*
- ► *how to reinforce your delivery with positive body language*
- ► *body language pitfalls.*

**Self-assessment**

1 When you stand up to speak, what should you do before you start your talk?

2 What are the greatest incentives for people to listen to you?

3 Name two things that can undermine a speaker.

4 What questions should you ask yourself before agreeing to speak?

5 What are the four Es?

6 Name two ways to make a talk lively.

7 Name two mannerisms to guard against when speaking.

8 What gives you confidence when speaking in public?

9 What is the maximum number of lines of text you should ideally have on a slide?

10 How can you make eye contact with as many of the audience as possible?

Answers are at the end of this chapter.

# How to prepare your talk

Most of us have to give a talk or make a speech at some time in our lives. It may be to a handful of colleagues or an audience of hundreds. The ability to put your point across in an interesting and informative way is essential, whether you are addressing a local charity committee or a business seminar. If the reason for the speech is social, then you may be able to decline being the speaker, but if it is related to your job you have no choice. Making presentations is now a part of most people's working lives, and it is vitally important to do this well. In today's competitive business world, those who can communicate with authority and confidence have a great advantage over their peers; good communicators are the ones who make it to the top.

Body language plays a crucial part in how we are perceived when we speak in public. Thorough preparation is the key to confidence, which enables us to use positive body language, which is as important as the content in making a success of public speaking.

**Key idea**

You do not want to be one of those of whom it is said: 'Before they get up they do not know what they are going to say; when they are speaking they do not know what they are saying; and when they sit down they do not know what they have said.'

Before you accept an invitation to speak, you need to ask a number of questions.

▶ Why? You will usually be asked to speak either because you are a good raconteur or because you are expert in a certain field. The latter should give you a degree of confidence because you already know your subject and much of the information is there in your head.

▶ Who? You need to know who you are talking to. Every speech, talk or presentation should be written with the audience in mind. What do your listeners want to know or need to hear? What do they know already? It sounds an obvious point to make, but it's surprising how many people stand up and say what they want to say, not what the audience wants or needs to hear!

▶ How many? What size is the audience and what age are they? What are their job categories or positions? Is it a mixed audience in terms of gender and culture, and if so, in what proportions. Being able to define your audience as accurately as possible will help you prepare a speech that will hit the spot and keep people interested.

▶ Where? The venue is important. Where is it and how long will it take to get there? How big is the room? If it is a large room with no microphone, is there a need for a sound system, and who will arrange this? If you are taking a laptop, is there a projector? Is there a flip chart or a lectern? Wherever possible, make sure you arrange all your presentation material yourself, and control as much of the presentation equipment as you can.

▶ What? You need to know the subject of the talk, and what the talk is to achieve. If the occasion is social, the subject might be left up to you. If the talk is work-related, the subject will probably be decided by the organizer, especially if it is given as part of a bigger event, such as a conference. If this is the case, you need to know what part it will have in the whole event and whether there will be any other speakers. The subject and the context of the talk will help you decide what the talk should aim to achieve – whether it is to inform, influence, recommend a course of action, persuade, motivate or entertain.

▶ How long? Do not be cajoled into speaking for any longer than your subject requires. It is always better to speak for a shorter time than to overrun. We all have busy schedules, and to waste people's valuable time is unacceptable.

### Key idea

The British prime minister Winston Churchill, who conquered a speech impediment to become a great orator, said of verbosity: 'It is sheer laziness not compressing thought into a reasonable space.'

All these questions need to be answered before you start to write your talk because if what you say isn't relevant, the audience won't bother to listen. Get as much information as you can from the organizers, whether they are clients, customers or people from your own company or department.

**WRITING YOUR TALK**

One of the things we all fear when we get up to speak is that we will forget everything we ever knew, including our own names! With careful preparation, however, we will not only remember everything we want to say, but also present our audience with all the relevant information in a logical, easily assimilated and entertaining way. It is easier to achieve this if you write out your talk in full. And give yourself time. Preparing any sort of presentation takes hours, not minutes.

Having found out why you are speaking and to whom, put yourself in their places. Try to answer the questions those people would ask. If you are addressing a group about specific difficulties – such as late deliveries – take the bull by the horns and mention it straightaway, telling them that you are aware of the problem and stating what you are doing to put it right. If people want a particular answer, they will not listen properly until you have satisfied their needs.

### Try it now

When starting to write a talk, it is a useful exercise to write down in one sentence the message you want your audience to take away with them. This helps to clarify your thoughts and makes your objective clear.

1 Think about the message.
2 Think about your audience.
3 If you could say only one sentence about your talk, what would it be?

Start off by writing down everything that could be relevant and of interest. Have a brainstorming session. Once you have decided what is relevant, write out a first draft. This is an important step towards getting the composition correct. It's so easy to think you know what you want and need to say, but unless the talk is structured properly, both you and the audience can get very confused. How many times have you heard speakers repeat themselves simply because they need thinking time, or have lost the direction of the talk?

However, it is very important to remember that you should write the talk to be spoken, not read! There is an enormous difference between how we hold someone's attention with the spoken word and how we hold it with the written word. When we speak to an audience, we have to use language that is easily understood. If our audience has to try too hard, they'll simply switch off.

The English language is one of the richest in the world, but we tend to use only a fraction of the words available to us. Don't try to sound as though you have swallowed a dictionary, but aim to make your talk as interesting as possible! Whatever your message, make it clear and concise.

One of the best ways to check how your talk will come across is to record yourself delivering it and play back the recording. Record yourself twice, first for the content, and when you are sure that's right, record the talk again for delivery. By listening to what you plan to say, you can:

▶ be sure you're not using the same 'pet' words repeatedly

▶ make certain your message is clear and to the point.

I would never advise anyone to learn a presentation word for word, but the better you know it, the more confident you will be. Many people like to put 'bullet points' on cards to prompt themselves about the main points of their talk. But even if you are planning to read the talk, it is still important to know it well, so that you can keep eye contact with your audience.

### Key idea

The human brain starts working the moment you are born and never stops until you stand up to speak in public.

### ▶ Opening remarks and introduction

It is often said that if you can't remember the introduction – it's too long! This is a pretty good rule of thumb. Keep the introduction short, as its purpose is to grab the attention of your audience. A quotation, a startling fact or an anecdote is a good way of getting people to listen to you.

### ▶ Structure

However you do it, the introduction is the first step down the road of your presentation, and you must make sure the audience stays with you all the way.

The introduction leads into your first key point. Having made a key point, back it up with sufficient detail to prove it, and then try to establish a brief but logical link to the next key point. For a short talk, try to keep to three or four clearly defined key points or subjects.

Opening remarks and introduction

First key point

Link

Second key point

Link

Third key point

Link

Conclusion

The aim is to lift your audience's interest with each point, rather like changing gear in a car.

Unless we perceive something to have relevance to us, we are not interested and tend not to listen, so you have to offer your audience something that they need or want to know – an incentive to listen. If your talk helps save your audience hassle, time or money, or shows them how to solve a problem, you will gain and keep their undivided attention!

The greatest incentives for anyone to listen to you are:

▶ fear

▶ benefit

▶ topicality

For instance, a key point about the introduction of a new computer system using the incentive of fear might be made as follows:

> 'The current system will be obsolete very shortly. It will cost a lot to maintain, and the longer we keep it the more costly it will become. The option I am recommending may seem expensive in the short term; however I believe that to secure the future we have no choice but to replace equipment that is going to be an increasing drain on our resources.'

The same key point might be made using the incentive of benefit:

> 'This new computer system may seem very expensive today, but the savings made in the cost of man hours alone will mean that it will have more than paid for itself by the start of the next financial year.'

Or the key point might be made using the incentive of topicality:

> 'As you may have seen in the press last week, the demand for faster, more efficient delivery schedules is increasing rapidly. Our company has to able to meet that demand, so I am recommending a new computer system to be implemented by the end of next month.'

The approach you use will depend on the audience and on what you want your talk to achieve.

### ▶ Keeping it lively

Paint pictures with words. Any phrases, sayings, anecdotes or analogies that you can use to illustrate a point will help an audience to understand something better than a bald fact. For instance, 'as heavy as a large suitcase' helps an audience understand the weight of something better than saying that it is 30 kilos. Similarly, 'as high as the Empire State Building' paints an immediate picture in our minds, which a number of feet or metres does not.

Obviously, this approach would not apply if you are giving a technical presentation where facts and figures have to be accurate. But descriptive phrases like the following enable listeners to identify with a situation you are describing:

> 'Solving the problem was like trying to stop a block of ice melting. Then we found the fridge.'

> 'The initial expenditure is going to cost no more than the price of an average family car.'

When you research your material, try to find some 'fascinating facts' that are not generally known. For example, if you were giving a talk about the history of afternoon tea, a question you could throw at the audience might be 'why do some people put the milk in before the tea, when others pour the tea in first?'. The fascinating fact would be that hot tea did not break bone china or porcelain cups but did crack clay or cheap china crockery, so those who could afford expensive crockery put the tea in first and those who could not put the milk in first.

If you are good at telling jokes, then by all means include some. However, don't try to be a stand-up comic; a joke that falls flat is far worse than no joke at all. Also bear in mind the journalists' golden rule: 'If in doubt, leave it out.' That also applies to any information you're unsure about.

### Key idea

Remember that very few people want to change places with you, as most of us dislike public speaking!

### ▶ The conclusion

This is a very important part of the talk. Summarize the major points, and make sure the audience knows when you have finished – if a speaker keeps saying 'and finally' or 'to summarize', the audience will switch off.

One useful way of concluding is to link back to something that you said in the introduction. Don't end with an apology; make sure the conclusion finishes the talk on a positive note.

#### TEAM PRESENTATIONS

When presenting as part of a team, it is vital to rehearse together so that material doesn't overlap and body language isn't contradictory. It is very important to support one another. Look interested when your colleagues are speaking no matter how many times you may have heard the presentation before – if you look bored or uninterested, your negative body language will transmit itself to the audience.

The team leader should introduce individual members and close the presentation by asking for questions or summarizing what has been said.

# How to deliver your talk

Once you have prepared the material, the next task is to present it.

It is best to stand when you are giving anything but a very informal talk. If you are standing, the members of the audience have to look up to you, and psychologically that gives you an advantage. Even in informal meetings it is a good thing to stand up, as it helps to overcome the natural vulnerability that we all feel when we are the focus of attention. But that is what you need to be when speaking in public. In order to get people to listen to you, their whole attention should be focused on you.

When you stand up to speak:

▶ wait for the audience to become quiet.

▶ stop, look round the room, and smile!

▶ introduce yourself if no introduction has been made.

Stopping and looking around for a moment before you begin to speak helps you to calm your nerves and assess your audience. A smile is one of the essential tools of body language, especially in public speaking. It is important for two reasons; it creates a bond with your audience, and it relaxes the muscles around the mouth, enabling you to use it properly. It also helps reassure the audience that they are in safe hands and are going to be given an interesting talk by a competent, confident presenter.

## THE FOUR E'S

The four vital elements to bring to any talk, whether it is long or short.

▶ Energy – no matter how tired you are or how many times you have given the talk, the same energy must be injected into your delivery. This comes from the voice as well as the body.

▶ Enthusiasm – enthusiasm comes through in your voice; and if you are not enthusiastic about your subject, why should anyone else be!

▶ Effort – a huge amount of effort must go into researching, preparing, writing and rehearsing your presentation.

▶ Enjoyment – this comes from knowing what you need to say and having prepared thoroughly so that you look forward to passing on the information.

## THE EIGHT P'S

It is not just what we say, but also the way we say it that makes people retain the message. When you speak in public, you need to use your voice and your body to help put over your message. The key aspects of delivering a talk can be summed up as the Eight Ps.

▶ Pace – speak a little more slowly than normal, as nerves tend to make our speech speed up, but don't speak at the same speed all the time; variations of speed keep the audience's attention better than a monotone!

▶ Pitch – speak at a slightly lower pitch than normal, as nerves tend to make our voice become higher-pitched, but avoid anything too low; aim for a pitch that feels comfortable. Try to vary your pitch as much as possible; this also adds 'colour' and interest to what you are saying.

▶ Phrasing – think about what you are saying and emphasize the points where the stress falls in a sentence. You will find out where these stresses fall when you rehearse; it can be a good idea to mark these in your written-out talk by underlining the relevant words.

▶ Projection – speak a little more loudly than normal, so that your words are clear and your voice carries to the back of the room, but without shouting. Produce your voice with plenty of controlled breathing.

▶ Pause – it is very important to pause every so often, preferably after making each key point in your talk. A pause gives your audience a chance to absorb what you are saying.

▶ Posture – You should stand upright and your body language should be relaxed. This is not just for appearance, but also because it's essential for correct breathing.

▶ Preparation – this is fundamental to feeling, and appearing, confident.

▶ Practice – writing your talk isn't the end of your preparation; you need to rehearse it as well. Only through rehearsal will you find out whether it is clear, logical and free from distracting mannerisms. Practice really does make perfect!

Two aspects of public speaking that can undermine a speaker are:

▶ running out of things to say

▶ equipment needed for the talk not working or not being there.

As mentioned earlier, speak for as long as your subject requires but then stop. If you start to waffle, body language such as throat-clearing, hand-wringing or shifting your feet will show that you are not comfortable with what you are saying.

If you need equipment to deliver some aspects of your talk, such as a laptop or projector, then wherever possible make the arrangements yourself for it to be present. You should also aim to control as much of the equipment yourself as you can. If something is missing or you are not operating it yourself, it creates an uncertainty that may show in nervous gestures that will undermine your authority.

## VISUAL AIDS

Visual aids are there to help the audience understand the message; they shouldn't be used simply as a prompt for the speaker. How many times have you seen people talking to the screen, sometimes turning their backs on the group they are addressing completely! Having said that, speakers (and their audiences) usually find that slides enliven a presentation. Graphs, charts and diagrams can be used to explain complex ideas and information, using PowerPoint or similar software.

Text slides emphasize the structure of a talk and lead the audience through the points the speaker wishes to cover. But never read directly from the words projected onto the screen, even if you are using the same words in your presentation. Your audience can do that for themselves, and it may make you look pompous, as if you think they aren't intelligent enough to read the words themselves. Illustrations used during a speech tell a story without the speaker having to give complicated information, reinforcing ideas and helping the audience stay involved.

There is really only one secret to good slides and that is simplicity. Each slide should be used to make one point only. Slides which contain too much information or illustration look cluttered and are difficult to follow. Too many words make the text small and difficult to read. As a general guideline it is best to have no more than six lines of text per slide and six words per line. Graphs and diagrams should be similarly uncluttered. If you feel that it is really important for your audience to have information in the form of complicated tables or diagrams, it is better to give them a hard copy in their conference papers, but don't give them out until the end of the talk. If people can read them beforehand, they might not bother to listen to you!

It is most effective to show approximately one slide every two minutes. You could use fewer than this, but more than this number would probably be too many for your audience.

**Remember this**

* Where will visual aids be used?
* What facilities are available there? If you are not sure, you must find out.
* How big/dark/light is the room?
* What is the message?
* Is it best conveyed in words or pictures?
* If very technical, would a handout be better?

The same principles apply to flipcharts. Keep the message simple. You cannot prepare clear visual aids until you are clear what the message is. It is as well to remember that audiences absorb surprisingly little! Use pictures to reinforce words.

**TAKING QUESTIONS**

If you take questions your presentation is not over; you are still 'under the spotlight'. A positive ending to a talk might go like this: 'I have given you all the information we have to date, so are there any questions?' If it is a large gathering it is a good idea to repeat the question that has been asked so that the rest of the audience is sure what has been asked. Look at the person who has asked the question as you start to answer and then expand it to the whole of the room. This is a time when you can expand on some points, but do not let yourself be dragged into a debate with a particularly argumentative person. If someone is very persistent and will not let a subject go, you could reply: 'As we have not got too much time I would like to move on, but let's meet afterwards so that we can get to grips with your specific problem.' If the last question is a negative one, try to finish with a positive point.

# Reinforcing your delivery with positive body language

The Eight Ps show the importance of body language and the voice in delivering a talk. However good the speech, if the body language doesn't match, the message will not be received as well as it should be. We cannot manufacture positive body language; it must look natural, and it should be unconscious. We have all seen politicians who have been told to look first this way, then that, and to raise and lower their hands at certain points in a speech, but this doesn't necessarily help them get their message across. Only genuine body language actually helps to emphasize points; it is something that should be spontaneous because when we know what we are saying, the body will do what it does naturally. Positive body language comes not only with the confidence of knowing we have prepared a good talk, but also from practising the talk with a view to working on our body language as well as the words.

As we discovered in Chapter 3, if a voice has no expression no one will listen to it, no matter how important the message; so it is vital that we learn to use the vocal range that we all possess to its full advantage. We can only use our voices well if we know how they sound – it really is vital to listen to your voice. The best way to do this is to record your voice and then analyse it.

 **Try it now**

* Read aloud something from a newspaper, record it and listen to it.
* Read a piece of poetry, record it, analyse it, then read it again using more expression.
* Read your talk, record it and listen to it.
* Do this at least three times.

Sound is caused by the breath striking the vocal cords. It is important to be as relaxed as possible. Tensing causes the breath to be shorter and the voice production poor.

Steady, regular breathing is vital to positive body language when giving a talk as it slows the heart rate as well as making you look and feel more confident.

**Try it now**

1 Expand your ribcage outwards and upwards, increasing the size of the chest.
2 The diaphragm descends and the chest increases, and more breath fills the lungs.
3 The diaphragm rises again while the ribs stay in the same position and air is expelled.
4 The ribs descend and further air is expelled.

It seems to be the act of standing that makes people most nervous when giving a talk or speech. The best way to conquer these nerves is to stand when you can. Even at informal meetings, stand to deliver your points. Your boss or colleagues may think it odd at first, but the more you get used to being in the 'spotlight' the easier it is to overcome nerves and keep negative body language under control. Just tell colleagues that you would like to stand when making your points or giving information.

**Try it now**

1 Stand tall with your head up. The fact that you are looking people in the eye will help you feel on a par with them.
2 Roll your shoulders up to your ears and then down until they rest naturally.
3 Pull your stomach in.
4 Tighten your buttocks.
5 Let your arms hang by your sides, keeping them behind the side-seams of your clothes. This helps keep your shoulders back.

Make eye contact with your audience. This can seem daunting, but it is the best way of engaging their attention. Don't look constantly in one direction; move your eyes around the room to engage as many people as possible. Try moving your eyes in a 'W' pattern, as this takes in more people and reaches all parts of the room.

Eye contact is also essential if you are to know how your audience is reacting. Learn to read the body language of an audience. If they are fidgeting, whispering or on their smartphones, you need to engage their attention more. You should be aiming to control your audience like a conductor directs an orchestra, building them up and bringing them down to keep their interest and attention.

## Body language pitfalls

It is just as crucial to avoid negative body language. Swaying, coughing, wringing the hands and similar mannerisms act as a distraction. If you are standing, place one foot slightly in front of the other as this will help you to keep reasonably still. However confident your voice may sound, if you are weaving like a snake in front of your audience you will not appear either confident or competent. Don't forget, you are the expert and your audience needs to be able to trust in your ability to deliver whatever it is that you are trying to tell them. This could be a product, a service, an idea or yourself. Whatever it is, you have got to put over the message in an interesting, informative and dynamic fashion, and that means being relaxed, prepared and confident.

## Remember this

* Don't shift from foot to foot
* Don't rub your nose or eyes
* Don't wander around
* Don't wring your hands
* Don't fiddle with cufflinks or jewellery
* Don't stroke your cheeks or chin
* Don't play with your hair
* Don't lose eye contact
* Don't scratch your bum!

These mannerisms are tell-tale signs that you are not as confident as you would like to be, so try to avoid them.

## Remember this: Delivery checklist

When you have delivered your talk, check these points:

* Was my purpose fulfilled? Did I impress, inform, convince?
* Was my message clear?
* Was my subject well-rehearsed?
* Did I complement the other speakers?
* Was my voice enthusiastic?
* Did I come across as sincere?
* Were my pauses used to good effect?
* Did my face show my feelings?
* Were my introduction and conclusion effective?
* Did I look natural?
* Was the rhythm of my speech good? Was it inconsistent or monotonous?
* Did I speak too slowly or too quickly?

If you didn't get it quite right this time, considering these points, and getting feedback from someone whose opinion you trust, will help you do better the next time.

## Key idea

'There are always three speeches, for every one you actually gave. The one you practised, the one you gave, and the one you wish you gave.'

Dale Carnegie

### Answers to self-assessment

1 Wait for the audience to become quiet; stop, look round the room, and smile; introduce yourself if no introduction has been made

2 Fear, benefit, topicality

3 Running out of things to say; equipment needed for the talk not being there or not working

4 Why, who, where, what, how many, how long

5 Energy, enthusiasm, effort, enjoyment

6 Paint pictures with words; use fascinating facts; use humour

7 Swaying; coughing; shifting from foot to foot; rubbing the nose or eyes; wandering around; wringing the hands; fiddling with cufflinks or jewellery; stroking your cheek or chin; playing with the hair; losing eye contact; scratching the bum

8 Thorough preparation

9 Six

10 Moving your eyes in a 'W' pattern.

### Focus points

The main points to remember from this chapter are:

✻ preparation is the key to confidence
✻ identify your audience
✻ get to know your voice
✻ get to know your body
✻ practise until you are perfect!

### Next step

**Chapter 8 will look at job interviews. It will cover preparation, suitable dress and the body language needed to help you make a good impression.**

# 8

# Interviews

**In this chapter you will learn:**

- ▶ *preparation*
- ▶ *what to wear*
- ▶ *interview skills*
- ▶ *telephone and Skype interviews.*

## Self-assessment

1 How quickly are interview decisions made, statistically speaking?

2 How important is proper preparation?

3 Name three signs of nervousness.

4 What are transferable skills?

5 How can you show empathy in a Skype interview?

6 Where should you sit in an interview?

7 Who should you look at in an interview?

8 What is 'active listening'?

9 What is an unsolicited CV?

10 What are the three Rs?

Answers are at the end of this chapter.

# Preparation

Different organizations look for different things when they are recruiting. Although a book like this can't go into all the different careers that are on offer, the information on creating a positive impression through your body language and visual image when being interviewed will enable you to make the best of yourself in what can be stressful circumstances.

There are several things that can make you stand out from other applicants:

► the way you present yourself in your CV and the job applications you make

► the way you present yourself visually

► the way you speak in public – see Chapters 3 and 7 for more details about this

► the way you handle an interview.

Applying for jobs may mean that you have to take a long, hard look at yourself. It can be a painful process, because no one likes to admit their shortcomings. But you must acknowledge them if you are going to project the positive image that's needed in today's competitive world.

**Try it now**

1 Write down your strengths and weaknesses.
2 Consider how you can build on your strengths.
3 Consider how you can overcome your weaknesses.

Many companies have difficulty filling positions with the right people, so they look closely at anyone with potential. However, the human resources staff who handle the initial stages of recruitment will often spend no longer than six seconds glancing at a CV. To stand out, it must be well-presented and contain something special on the first page. If there is an accompanying letter, it should try to show your personality and be interesting and attention-grabbing, but not flippant. Put yourself in the employer's position as much as possible. They are looking for transferable skills that have been gained from a number of different activities; it is not the fact that you joined the basketball team but how you contributed that is significant for them. If you can't give an indication of what your transferable skills are, then in an employer's eyes you haven't gained anything from the experience. A good example of this would be: 'I organized an away match for the amateur football club I belong to. It involved hiring a coach, booking the train tickets and liaising with the Belgian team before the match.'

An unsolicited CV accompanied by a carefully constructed email or letter can be successful because it is not up against the same competition as when a job has been advertised. Even in times of a depressed labour market, employers might look kindly at someone who shows this sort of initiative.

Since the downturn in the global economy began in 2008, working life has become very uncertain. Many graduates have found that they are over-qualified for the jobs on offer and face the dilemma of whether to mention all their qualifications. If an employer sees a masters degree or an MBA on someone's CV and that level of qualification is not needed for the job, they may think the candidate will expect too high a salary or will quickly get bored with the job and move on. If you attend interviews for such jobs, it is crucial your body language is not arrogant or over-confident, so active listening skills should be employed.

Companies also recognize the value of experience, and there is a feeling that if someone has done a particular job well for other companies, they will work well for them too. Experience can mean different things to different people. Someone who has been in a managerial position for 18 months may be just as capable as someone who has been in the same position for five years; in fact they may be a better candidate, as people can become stale after being in a job for a certain length of time. If you wish to change jobs and have been in your current position for a significant length of time, it is important to say why you have stayed and what both you and the company have gained as a result; then say why you are leaving.

Redundancy is a traumatic experience even if a substantial redundancy payment has relieved immediate financial worries, so the effort to recreate a positive image can be hard; when you are in the pit it can be difficult to climb out. Self-motivation is vital and the most important thing for more mature applicants is to identify skills that are transferable from the job they have left to organizations where those skills will provide added value.

Beyond qualifications and experience, there are certain qualities that are needed for almost any job:

▶ resourcefulness

▶ resilience

▶ responsibility

▶ vision.

These qualities are relatively easy to identify and if people have had previous jobs, there is usually evidence to show that they possess these.

▶ Resourcefulness helps people to find ways around a problem and to seek out solutions to problems themselves. If an employer gives you a project, he or she does not want you to come back every five minutes asking what to do.

▶ Resilience sees people through in the long term. It is a combination of stamina, being able to cope with the politics of an organization, and the ability to overcome barriers and persevere without giving up. Employers need people who are good at coping with change. Companies look for those who can introduce change. As key people, they have to be agents of change.

▶ Responsibility is self-evident from a few well-chosen questions. What do you do in your spare time? What projects have you been responsible for? How much did you contribute to the running of the department?

▶ Vision is also very important – to be successful you need to have vision. Changes in management and in the business environment are the norm today, so the ability to see learning and development as part of your own responsibility is indispensable. To be curious is part of survival; never take things for granted and never be afraid to ask the question 'Why?'.

### Key idea

'About 15 per cent of one's financial success is due to one's technical knowledge and about 85 per cent is due to skill in human engineering, to personality and the ability to lead people.'

Dale Carnegie

### Remember this

* First impressions – your CV should be well-presented and interesting
* Relevant experience – draw out past experience that is relevant to the job
* Necessary skills – draw out your transferable skills
* Reason for applying – give positive reasons for why you are interested in the job, and why you want to leave your current position
* Preparation – research the organization and the role.

Comprehensive research is essential. If you do not know what a company does, you will not impress at an interview; if you do not know what a company is like, you cannot know whether you would like to work for it; and if you do not know what a job involves, you do not know whether you would enjoy doing it. For instance, if you are very ambitious, a small business might not provide scope for the promotion that you are looking for, so think carefully about what you want and look for a position in a company or organization that is right for you.

### Remember this

Research the organization:

* What does it do? Who does it serve?
* Who owns it? What is its market?
* Who are the key personnel?
* How many people does it employ?
* What is its reputation?
* Is the annual turnover increasing or decreasing?

The next thing is to look at the job description very carefully.

### Remember this

* What is the job title?
* What is its purpose?
* What are the terms and conditions?
* How will the job develop?

Now think about yourself. How would you like somebody to describe you after a first meeting?

### Try it now

1 Write down three adjectives describing yourself.
2 Analyse what you have written.

One word might be 'enthusiastic'; if so, make sure that side of your personality comes across in your interview. If 'hardworking' is another of the words, consider what evidence you could present of a project that you have worked on. Write down other characteristics and see if they match up with the job description. Consider how you can demonstrate these qualities to a prospective employer.

It is essential to prepare for an interview and to start in plenty of time. By the time you are panicking, it's too late!

Always be positive! Try to envisage the best possible outcome of a situation. If you think you are going to fail at an interview you are much more likely to do so; if you expect to be successful, then provided you have done your preparation you are much more likely to land the job.

**Try it now**

✷ Visualize positive outcomes.
✷ Discard negative thoughts.
✷ Build on your strengths.

## What to wear

Recognized qualifications and relevant skills and experience are prerequisites for any job, but equally essential is that the first impression you make is a positive one. Bearing in mind the number of applicants applying for most appointments these days, you only have a few minutes to make your mark, to create a positive image.

A prospective employer will make an instant decision about whether you're a tidy or untidy person, imaginative or chic, based on your appearance. Men usually get more time to create an impression, as interviewers will wait to hear what they have to say before coming to a judgement, whereas women, unfortunately, are more likely to be judged on the first impression created by their clothes. Even if you cannot afford expensive clothes, you can still make a good impression if your clothes, shoes and accessories are clean, well cared for and tidy.

When you go for a job interview it's important to look the part, but it is also vital not to dress or talk yourself out of the job before you start. Think of the impression you are giving a potential new boss. If you behave as though you are after the boss's job and dress as if you are a member of the board, it might not go down well. Equally, it wouldn't do to look as though you have just got out of bed and put on the first thing that came to hand.

Almost every business, organization or public body will, whether it admits it or not, have its own 'stamp', i.e. the dress code, physical appearance and manner in which it expects an employee to act, and the image it looks for in the ideal employee. If that image is not for you, then you are unlikely to be happy working in that organization. How you dress is important not only for an interview but also when you start the job. We should not try to be what we are not, and if wearing a suit every day is something that will make you feel stifled and uncomfortable, then your body language will show this and you should think seriously about whether you want the position. You may think if you dress in a certain way you are showing that you are an individual with an unusual mind, but the message received might be of somebody who is a loner, a potentially difficult person who will not fit in. Inadvertently you could be giving off the wrong signals to a potential employer, or your boss if you're looking for promotion.

Colours are important. Wearing colours that enhance your skin tone can make the difference between you looking healthy and vibrant or tired and washed out. The style of dress makes an immediate impression, and this is especially true for women. Unfortunately, as we get older, people seem to think we lose our senses as well as our looks, assuming that if our clothes are out of date our ideas probably are too! This doesn't happen as much to men and it is as untrue for women as it is unfair, but it does mean that it is important to move with the times in the way you dress.

It's wise to look at a corporate image very carefully, because it will tell you not only how you should dress, but also the way you are expected to behave and the type of people you will be working with. If you go for an interview wearing a hijab or kilt, say, this will have an effect on the interview – the first impression might be one of doubt about whether you will fit in culturally with the organization – so think carefully about the company culture as well as the job itself. This advice extends also to body decoration such as piercings or tattoos; it might not matter to an interviewer if you happen to have a ring through your nose, or it might be a serious issue because it is contrary to company policy. It could be deemed unsafe, unsuitable or in some other way inappropriate for that particular workplace.

# Interview skills

Handling yourself well in interviews might help you achieve not only a job but also a position you want in a voluntary organization, such as being elected to the local council or the board of governors of your children's school, or becoming the chair of your golf club. Statistically, interview decisions are made within the first 60 seconds of meeting someone, often before the candidate has even opened his or her mouth! How you are dressed, how you walk, how you shake hands and your overall body language go to form a positive or negative image.

A successful interview will flow, and you should aim to achieve a good rapport with your interviewer. A good start is to smile as you enter the room. Once seated, make sure you sit up straight, as it makes you look more alert – slouching does not make a good impression. Try to make sure that you are sitting with your body at an angle of 45 degrees to your interviewer, to create empathy with them rather than a sense of confrontation. Mirroring body language can also be very effective in this respect, but make sure it is not contrived as most interviewers are experienced in reading body language. If they steeple their hands and you immediately do the same, and then change position as soon as they do, it can become a rather distracting game! Like all body language, the more natural it is, the better.

There are a number of negative body language signs that affect someone who is nervous, such as a dry mouth, licking the lips, throat clearing, foot tapping, hand wringing, head scratching and rapid breathing. Try to control or avoid these, as they will not make a good impression. A firm, positive handshake is vital, and makes a strong impression on the person you are meeting, but take your signal from the interviewer. Although walking in and offering your hand can look very confident, I suggest you do not proffer a hand unless prompted, as you do not want to be seen as teaching someone their manners. If you have not shaken hands by the end of the interview, then by all means take the initiative.

Eye contact with your interviewer or interviewers is critical. If your interview is in front of a panel, look at the person who asked the question before making eye contact with the others and then coming back to the original questioner at the end of your answer. Include everyone there, as you don't know who is going to make the final decision.

Respond to the person who asked the question even if that person is busy writing notes; they are still listening. Listening skills are essential for you too; an interview can be thrown off-course if you answer the question you thought you heard rather than the one that was asked. It sounds obvious, but it's surprising how many people, usually through nerves, rush into an answer. Listen not only to the question, but also to the inflection used when asking the question.

## Phone and Skype interviews

These days, a first interview in the job recruitment process is likely to be over the phone, especially for international appointments, so Chapters 6 and 10 are also relevant here.

However practical it may be to interview by phone or Skype in some circumstances, such interviews present their own problems. The Canadian Red Cross does a lot of interviews by Skype and phone as candidates are located all over the world. Joan Gibley, the organization's senior financial analyst, finds there are drawbacks to interviewing via Skype. 'A lot is lost over Skype because you can't read the body language easily and decide whether you would like to work with the person or not,' says Joan. 'The interviews are not as natural. You don't connect like in a face-to-face interview.'

So how you can you improve the sense of connection via Skype or the phone? Leaning forward and nodding your head (active listening), as well as keeping eye contact with the camera will help to make the interview more personal.

### Remember this

＊ Make sure you wear something that projects the image you want to project

＊ Choose the location carefully, as your surroundings will be noted

＊ Practise active listening

＊ Look into the camera to establish eye contact.

The impression a person, a place or an organization makes on you is very important when deciding whether to take the job. However, beware of jumping to snap decisions, especially about people. Some of us are better at evaluating people than others, and although you should take notice of initial reactions, they should not prejudice you against exploring further. This is particularly the case if you are taking part in a selection process for a position. A candidate for a teaching post may not initially give the impression that he or she could control a class of unruly adolescents. Further investigation, however, could show that they have proved more than a match for the situation in the past and are exactly right for the job. So look at the overall picture rather than focusing on one particular aspect.

### Answers to self-assessment

1 Within 60 seconds of meeting someone

2 Very important; do your homework before the interview

3 Lip-licking; throat-clearing; foot-tapping; hand-wringing; head scratching; rapid breathing

4 Things learnt in one job that will be valuable in another

5 By leaning forward and nodding

6 At a 45 degree angle to your interviewer

7 At the interviewer or interviewers

8 Nodding and leaning towards the speaker

9 A CV that is sent in speculatively, i.e. not in response to a job advertisement

10 Resourcefulness, reliance and responsibility

### Focus points

The main points to remember from this chapter are:

* do your research
* smile as you walk into the room
* sit up straight and maintain eye contact
* listen carefully
* ask relevant questions.

## Next step

**The next step is to examine different job sectors and analyse the attributes most employers are looking for. Chapter 9 will show you how positive body language can help you to get that job.**

# 9

# What employers want

In this chapter you will learn about the qualities and the image required by:

- ▶ *graduates*
- ▶ *the professions*
- ▶ *industry*
- ▶ *theatre, television and film*
- ▶ *journalism*
- ▶ *the armed services, security and police*
- ▶ *the medical profession, social workers and carers*
- ▶ *the teaching profession*
- ▶ *sales*
- ▶ *hospitality and customer service*
- ▶ *university and college applicants.*

## Self-assessment

1 What are life skills?

2 How important is enthusiasm for a job?

3 Why is work experience significant?

4 Name two of the qualities needed in the teaching profession.

5 How can you build on your strengths?

6 What is important in any job?

7 How should you choose clothes for an interview?

8 What qualities are needed in a good salesperson?

9 What do employers want to see in a graduate?

10 How can you make yourself stand out?

Answers are at the end of this chapter.

# Graduates

The job market for those leaving college and university has intensified in recent years. The interview is all important, as it sometimes takes place before you sit your final exams. If you fail your finals, you may not be taken on; but if you have done a good interview, less importance may be placed on the class of degree you have achieved. Use your university's careers service, as it should be able to give you help and guidance, and all companies work closely with them. In most cases, the careers service is staffed by professionals who know the companies and can send you to a workshop that will help you improve your interviewing skills if you are concerned that these might let you down. People do want to see your personality during an interview, but they will only see the image that you project. If you say you are bright and cheery, then there must be evidence to suggest that you are!

Academic achievements are important, although not necessarily so – ask Bill Gates! But an application from someone with no interests outside their academic studies and/or no work experience will often be immediately rejected by many companies. Just having been to university is not enough; for many jobs the employer is looking for something more. So think about what non-academic achievements and experience might give you added value and make you stand out from other candidates. This need not be a great feat like running a marathon or climbing Mount Everest, but the fact that you can type 80 words a minute, even though the job might not require that particular skill, may sway a decision in your favour.

Drawing up such a list of achievements and experiences will help you create a positive image of yourself, and a positive image will show in positive body language. Your abilities might include being able to cook, sew or drive, having a good knowledge of IT or speaking a foreign language, as well as being able to spell correctly and being numerate. Holiday jobs and travel can also contribute to your list, especially if they are relevant to the job. And don't overlook the less immediately obvious. For instance, if you were the eldest child of working parents and had to look after younger siblings, you probably have an inbuilt sense of responsibility that would be valuable for any job in a supervisory capacity. Experience of dealing with cantankerous, ageing relatives would enable you to cope with difficult customers or patients. But how often would you think of mentioning experience like this on your CV?

A standard question from students is, 'Can you tell me more about the company's training and development policy?' Although this shows a commendable desire to progress while remaining with the company, if you ask a question that shows you have thoroughly researched the company, it will make a much greater impression on the interviewer. For example, the question 'My interest is software development. Is that likely to be increased by the multimedia work the company is doing?' shows an understanding of the nature of the business. The more specific you can be, the more profitable the line of interviewing will be, as it indicates a focus on the part of the applicant. It is also important to read the newspapers and relevant trade magazines as part of your research.

Even if you don't ask a question based on your research into the company, you might be asked to tell the interviewer what you know about the organization. So don't skimp on the research. If you flounder with an obvious question like this, it will show in your body language and severely undermine your credibility.

Once you start shifting in your seat, touching your face or fiddling with your hands, your interviewer will be on the alert for any other signs of insecurity rather than listening to what you are saying.

## The professions

Life in all the professions has changed enormously since the beginning of the 21st century and competition for jobs in the professions is on the increase. The number of graduates coming out of university each year far outnumbers the number of vacancies available, and yet many organizations say that they have difficulty finding the 'right' people. So what will make you the right person? If you are going to choose a career in one of the professions – accountancy, banking, chartered surveying, insurance, the law, to name but a few – you will probably need a degree and specific professional qualifications, and certain qualities:

- ▶ leadership
- ▶ motivation
- ▶ determination
- ▶ enthusiasm
- ▶ good team player
- ▶ loyalty
- ▶ ambition
- ▶ integrity
- ▶ hard working
- ▶ conscientious
- ▶ initiative
- ▶ drive
- ▶ ability to learn a language.

Dress in the professions is usually fairly conservative, although there are exceptions. Your clothes do not have to be expensive – high street stores will meet your needs – but they do need to be classic, discreet, elegant and smart to meet the requirements of most professions that do not have a uniform. Bright colours are fine – they make you stand out – but you have to be aware that you are drawing attention to yourself.

## Remember this

The following applies to most professional careers, and many office-based jobs.

* Buy clothes that you can mix and match.
* Choose materials that will wear well and won't crease too easily.
* Buy the most expensive clothes you can comfortably afford.
* Sober colours are better.
* Dress to suit everybody – a middle-of-the-road style – so that you don't offend anybody.
* Make sure shoes, briefcases and handbags are kept in good condition.
* You are the image of your organization – look professional!

# Industry

What academic qualifications you need will depend on what sector of industry you wish to work in, but generally speaking a science-based degree will open far more doors than an arts degree.

A science background trains prospective managers in a logical method of thinking and enables them to look at situations objectively, showing flair and imagination, especially in problem-solving. Many larger companies are meticulous in their search for new staff. They do the 'milk round' at universities and are constantly thinking of new ways to attract the right graduates. Many companies don't select new employees on academic qualifications alone, although qualifications are obviously important when it comes to work in technical areas. For work in a non-technical area, companies look for other qualities too, such as innovation, determination and communication skills, making the nature of the qualification less important.

The qualities needed for work in industry usually include:

- technical knowledge
- leadership
- motivation
- determination
- communication skills
- the ability to work as part of a team
- attention to detail.

The importance of dress varies depending on a company's clientele and the level of contact the employee has with customers. If a job means someone will meet customers, especially substantial customers, appearance will be important and should be professional. But for a technical job that doesn't involve meeting the public, dress is not so significant.

## Theatre, television and film

The image of this professional world is one of glamour, high earnings and 'arty' types of people. It does have its glamorous side, and a small percentage of actors do earn huge amounts of money, and it certainly has its share of characters. The reality, though, is a tough, overcrowded and precarious occupation. However, if it is in your blood and there is no other way you want to earn your living, then it can be the most exciting profession in the world. But it is essential to be realistic about both your ability and your dedication.

If you are going to succeed in the theatre, then ideally you should be able to sing, dance and play at least one instrument; television and films are different. On stage you have to create the part; in films and on TV you have to look the part.

When a director holds auditions, they generally decide quickly who they want for a role. It helps if somebody projects an image and has looks that are right for the part. Because rehearsal periods are usually so short that there is no time to work on creating the character, the director needs an actor who is as near to the character as possible. Body language is crucial here; if you can 'think' yourself into the character, your body language will define that character. As television and film rely on the visual image more than dialogue, analysing the body language of many different types of people and storing it in your memory is essential.

The film and television industries have an enormous number of people applying for jobs. Film companies tend to be formed anew for each production, which can take well over a year to complete, and so everyone is effectively freelance. The television industry is now heading in much the same direction, with fewer permanent posts and more people employed on long- or short-term contracts. For most television jobs, applicants now require a degree, although it tends not to matter what the subject is. However, IT and computer skills are essential.

The smaller independent production companies look for enthusiasm. People must be keen, not afraid of a challenge or long hours, and be prepared to tackle the unusual. The most important thing is to be able to work as part of a team, especially in a small organization.

The technical posts each require their own level of education. Knowledge of relevant equipment is vital, and it is a good idea to put together a short show-reel of programmes you have worked on. If you have not worked before, it is essential to have samples of your projects, such as a portfolio of photographs or a video, for example, if you are going for a camera operator's job. Bear in mind that in a small organization yours might be the only face that the customer, client or viewer sees, so it is crucial to present a good public image; you may then be remembered and invited back again to film. Even the best camera operator or sound recordist in the world will not be employed by some companies if he or she looks a mess.

The qualities needed for work in theatre, television and film usually include:

▶ imagination

▶ motivation

- determination
- enthusiasm
- tenacity
- ambition
- ability to cope with the knocks
- proficiency in mannerisms, voices and accents
- observational skills
- being able to work on a production and deal with people at all levels sensitively but firmly
- ability to work long hours
- 100 per cent dedication.

Appearance should look creative but professional. If you are an actor, look the part!

## Journalism

Probably the most important quality for a journalist is curiosity, followed by the skill to ask incisive questions and the ability to make a story different, to make it stand out in such a way that people will notice it.

Journalism is also an overcrowded profession, with less job security than there used to be. But if this is the job for you, use your time at school or college to write as many articles as you can get people to read! Practice does make perfect. Work experience is vital, so volunteer to work unpaid at the company where you would like a job. If the unpaid work is done well, you stand a good chance of getting a job there if a vacancy arises.

The qualities needed for work in journalism usually include:

- motivation
- energy
- enthusiasm
- curiosity

- IT skills

- organizational skills

- observational skills

- ability to work long hours.

Your appearance should be neat, tidy and professional; remember you are the public face of the organization you work for.

# The armed services, security and police

People in these jobs must look professional and competent. Both your body language and your visual image have to show that you are a disciplined and organized individual. By this I mean you have to walk tall, stand and sit straight, and look alert. You have to look as though you can look after yourself, take orders and conform, but you also have to show that you can listen. Body language is crucial here, active listening during an interview is critical as it will be part of your job. Asking relevant but incisive questions can show you are able to take the initiative, but never try to out-smart your interviewer!

The qualities needed for this work usually include:

- 100 per cent dedication

- motivation

- energy

- enthusiasm

- organizational skills

- ability to work long hours

- ability to cope with challenges

- observational skills

- listening skills

- attention to detail

- being able to take orders.

Appearance must be smart and professional, with clothes in immaculate condition and shoes well-polished. Hair should be tidy and off the face.

## The medical profession, social workers and carers

People in these professions must come across as professional but caring. Both the way you dress and your body language must inspire confidence. Active listening when seeing patients or clients is an essential part of the work, so demonstrating these skills at an interview is important.

The qualities needed in the medical and caring professions usually include:

▶ 100 per cent dedication

▶ motivation

▶ energy

▶ excellent listening skills

▶ empathy and compassion

▶ organizational skills

▶ ability to work long hours

▶ ability to cope with challenges

▶ observational skills

▶ attention to detail.

It is vital to dress well, and to look both healthy and in control. No one wants to see a doctor, nurse, physiotherapist, social worker or carer who looks scruffy – the immediate unconscious thought would be: 'If they can't look after themselves, they can't look after me.' No one wants to see a medic who looks worse than they feel! Remember, they are putting their most precious thing in your hands – their life.

# The teaching profession

Teaching today is a very demanding job. In some parts of the UK, up to 70 different languages may be spoken in a school. To engage with so many diverse cultures and levels of English is quite a challenge.

In addition to the linguistic and cultural variety, teachers have to deal with the sometimes challenging behaviour of students. Margaret Fraser, a teacher for many years, has seen huge behavioural changes in the classroom. 'Negotiation rather than discipline is the norm in many schools now,' says Margaret. 'In order to gain control of the class you have to present a really positive image. Confident body language is a must, because if they see you are lacking in confidence you've got no chance of getting or keeping their attention however well you know your subject.'

How you dress is significant too, in Margaret's opinion. 'The students are summing you up as much as you are assessing them, and if you look well-groomed, trendy and up to the minute, you are much more likely to gain their respect than if you look as though you couldn't care less.' Margaret also rates enthusiasm as being essential in teaching anybody anything, and keeping yourself enthused in often challenging circumstances is vital. Body language and the visual image can really help in the way you are perceived by your students and therefore how they react to you. Show them the respect of caring how you present yourself and you should find that you gain some respect in return.

The qualities needed in the teaching profession usually include:

▶ dedication

▶ motivation

▶ energy

▶ patience

▶ tenacity

▶ listening skills

▶ empathy and compassion

- organizational skills
- ability to cope with challenges
- observational skills
- attention to detail.

## Key idea

'Whether you think you can or think you can't – you are right.'

Henry Ford

# Sales

You need to like people, have self-confidence and be thoroughly motivated to be a good salesperson. It is often a gift. You can teach someone what to say and how to say it, but reading body language is fundamental if you are to be successful. Allan Pease, an acknowledged body language expert, tells how he became a highly successful salesman by learning to assess the body language of his customers when he was selling rubber sponges door-to-door after school at the age of eleven. 'When I knocked on a door, if someone told me to go away but their hands were open and they showed their palms, I knew it was safe to persist because they weren't aggressive. If someone told me to go away in a soft voice but used a pointed finger or closed hand, I knew it was time to leave.' Maureen Oakden was a senior sales consultant with an international pharmaceutical company selling medicines to doctors' surgeries. 'I could usually tell as soon as I walked into the room whether the buyers were interested or not. If they didn't get up to meet me or even ask me to sit down, I knew I was going to have to work hard to get their attention. I would wait until he or she looked up from their computer and immediately thank them for seeing me and get straight down to business. If they didn't want the product they certainly didn't want me to waste their time.' Because Maureen read their body language, she never antagonized a client and so was always welcome back.

The qualities needed in sales usually include:

► 100 per cent dedication

► motivation

► energy

► listening skills

► confidence

► organizational skills

► capacity to work long hours

► ability to turn challenges into opportunities

► observational skills

► attention to detail.

Appearance must be smart and professional.

## Hospitality and customer service

With hospitality and customer service I am including hotel, restaurant, airline and retail staff. Unfortunately, some people in this vital sector are poorly paid, so staff turnover is a serious problem for many businesses. Even if working in a cafe or shop is only a holiday job, you will gain valuable customer service experience, which will help you in any future job that involves dealing with the public – which, in fact, is most jobs. Do any job to your best ability, even if it is cleaning the washrooms, and you will do it well. A job well done is noticed and can lead to promotion. When I was in Nairobi recently, one of the delegates on my training course worked for Kenya Airways. She had very little education and had started as a cleaner, with her main job being to clean the aircraft toilets – something no one else was very keen to do! She realized that not only did the job need doing, it needed doing properly, so she always volunteered. After a while, the management noticed not only her dedication, but also her cheerfulness when working. She has been made a supervisor, and was sent on our corporate awareness course because she is being promoted to management level.

Coping with difficult clients and customers needs good diplomatic skills, and body language that reinforces these. When you are on duty, it is essential to look interested at all times. Leaning against a wall, slumping in your seat or resting elbows on the desk is negative body language and will be noticed, as will chatting to other members of staff while ignoring customers.

The qualities needed in hospitality and customer service usually include:

► motivation

► enthusiasm

► being a good team player

► loyalty

► conscientiousness

► ability to take orders

► capacity to work long hours

► attention to detail

► a smile!

In this sector, workers may be required to wear a uniform. If there is no uniform, dress is usually quite conservative, with a few exceptions. Your clothes do not have to be expensive – they could come from high street stores – but they should be classic in style, discreet, elegant and smart. Bright colours are fine, but they make you stand out, so you should be aware that you are drawing attention to yourself.

The above tips are applicable for most professional careers, or indeed any office-based job.

# University and college interviews

Everything that is applicable to dressing for a job interview is also applicable to university and college interviews, as the course you take will, in many cases, lead to a job in a particular sector. Higher education is relatively expensive now so you want to make sure you go to the best college or university for your discipline. As funding for these institutions is based on their results, they will choose students who are motivated, intelligent and look as though they will succeed, so confident body language is essential. Smile as you walk into the room. Sit up straight. Maintain eye contact. Ask relevant questions, but never try to outsmart your interviewer. Listen carefully and show that you are listening by nodding your head occasionally.

## Remember this

- Hobbies, sports and previous experience are all important if they will add value to the job you are eventually seeking.
- Transferable skills must be relevant. Amateur dramatics or chairmanship of the debating society would be good experience for a salesperson or a teacher, but not particularly relevant if you want to be a computer programmer.
- Be careful how you word things. If you are captain of a sports team, it probably means you are good with people, but too much involvement in sport might suggest to an interviewer that you have not concentrated fully on your work.
- Ask yourself 'What did I actually do?' There is no point in saying 'we did this' and 'we decided that' if there is no evidence to prove that it was you who initiated anything.
- Make sure your clothes are appropriate for the course you are applying for.
- Ensure hair is tidy, nails are clean and you look healthy and rested.

Why is your personal image so important? If you look as though you never sleep, don't eat properly and party all night you will not project the image of someone who is prepared to work hard and learn. If crumpled clothes and casual body language appear to confirm this, interviewers are more likely to give the place to someone they think really wants it and is prepared to work hard.

The qualities needed in university and college interviews usually include:

- enthusiasm
- motivation
- energy
- organizational skills
- ability to collate and assimilate information
- ability to cope with challenges
- observational skills
- attention to detail.

Appearance must be tidy, appropriate for the profession the course might lead to, healthy and alert!

## Answers to self-assessment

1 Things you learn in everyday life

2 Vital

3 Because it helps increase knowledge and gives you an idea of the job you might want

4 Dedication, motivation, energy, patience, tenacity, listening skills, empathy, compassion, organizational skills, ability to cope with challenges, observational skills, attention to detail

5 By identifying them and working to improve them

6 Motivation

7 By identifying company culture

8 Confidence and motivation

9 Personality as well as academic achievements

10 With a good CV, a positive image and confident body language.

## Focus points

The main points to remember from this chapter are:

* do your research
* smile as you walk into the room
* sit up straight
* maintain eye contact
* listen carefully
* ask relevant questions.

## Next step

**The media can be a source of free PR or the destroyer of a company's reputation. Like it or loathe it, the media is important to any business. Chapter 10 will show you how the media works and what you can do to use it to your best advantage.**

# 10

# The media

In this chapter you will learn about:

▶ *types of interview*
▶ *body language in television interviews*
▶ *body language in radio interviews*
▶ *body language in press interviews.*

## Self-assessment

1 Why is it important to sit up straight?

2 Where should you look when you are being interviewed?

3 What is a good interview?

4 Should you ever talk off the record?

5 When should you refuse to comment?

6 What should you do when talking to a press journalist over the phone?

7 What is 'the notebook ploy'?

8 Why should you cultivate the press?

9 What colours should you avoid wearing on television?

10 Name two types of interview.

Answers are at the end of this chapter.

# Broadcast interviews

### TYPES OF INTERVIEW

There are different types of interview and you must prepare appropriately for each.

### ▶ The informative interview

Clarity is essential. Decide the main point you wish to put over and then make your subordinate points in descending order of importance. This means that if the interview is cut short for some reason, only the less important points will be lost.

Not only should the most important point be made first, it should be made again, if possible, part way through the interview, and a final re-statement is helpful if the message is significant enough. Keep a final re-statement to just a few words, however, because ending comments can often be cut, even in mid-sentence, if time has run out.

Since the point of this type of interview is to elicit information, the interviewer should have little objection to discussing the questions with you in advance. Don't expect too much in terms of air-time. Although your subject is of paramount importance to you, and hopefully to a wider audience, it has to fit into a busy programme schedule. Two to three minutes is the usual length of this type of interview.

If you have any pictures or video to illustrate your subject, take them to the television studio with you but do mention them well in advance. The director has enough to do while the programme is being recorded or broadcast and will not upset production plans at the last moment for your visual aids. If you speak to the broadcasting company beforehand, you give them the chance to use the material to the best advantage, thereby helping your explanation of your subject.

This type of interview is usually painless, unless nerves reduce you to a jelly-like state. Careful preparation is the best way to overcome this problem. Always consider your performance and approach from the audience's point of view. What they need to hear is far more important than what you might enjoy telling them.

### ▶ The critical interview

This is, unfortunately, the type of interview most people are likely to undergo. Preparation is essential, coupled with an absolute mastery of your subject. And again, consider your subject from the audience's point of view; this should be a good pointer to the questions you are likely to be asked. In all probability, your interviewer knew little about your subject yesterday and is unlikely to know much about it tomorrow, but today he or she is as big an expert as you are. The interviewer, or their researchers, will have found out the key facts and will have a very clear idea of the line that the questioning will take. You will not be told in advance what those questions will be, but the areas for discussion should be established before an interview of this kind. It is as well to be aware that some interviewers may have spent weeks researching your interview, so beware of any skeletons in your cupboard!

Make clear in advance any areas that you are not prepared to discuss – you are quite within your rights to do this. There have been cases where a lack of liaison between researcher, producer and interviewer has resulted in questions being asked that the interviewee did not expect and is either unable or unwilling to answer. The resulting embarrassment for the interviewee can lead to an unconvincing answer and uncomfortable body language. This is not in anybody's best interests. If, despite everything, you are asked a question you are unable to answer, say straight out that it is a topic about which you are not qualified to speak. If you received an assurance some aspect of the subject would not be touched upon, don't be afraid to say so if the interviewer does not respect this assurance. Then sit back and leave your interviewer to get out of the mess without your aid.

Should this type of interview descend into a contest, short answers do much to discomfort an interviewer, although it would be dangerous to carry this to an extreme. Here, preparation assumes even greater importance. Having decided where the attack might come from and the form it will take, work out the shortest satisfactory answer, as this will prove the most manageable line to defend. Having established your line, stick to it. Do not fall for the well-known ploy of the interviewer listening sympathetically, maybe even nodding kindly, and then saying nothing when you stop talking. A steady gaze in the eye, giving you the impression that what you are saying is riveting, might tempt you to go on. If you do, you could find yourself in trouble. Resist the temptation to break the silence. The pause may last a second or two, but although to you it may feel like a lifetime, it is best to return the interviewer's 'kindly' gaze and keep your mouth shut. The ball is in the interviewer's court. Leave it there. Body language is crucial here, as an experienced journalist or presenter will be looking out for any signs of nervousness or unease.

Do not try the politician's game of answering a different question from the one you have been asked. It invites the retaliation, 'Very good answer, but I wonder if you would now answer the question I put to you.' This is an undignified position for the interviewee as well as putting the viewer immediately on the side of the interviewer. From then on, everything you say will have less impact and is unlikely to be well-received by the audience.

If the interviewer has got you on the spot, admit it; not all of it, but as much as suits you. Replies on the lines of 'I've got to admit there's a lot in what you say. We have made mistakes. But we've learnt from them and it won't happen again' can be helpful. Having partially proved the point, the interviewer is likely to move on to another subject, leaving any real skeletons still safely in your cupboard. Added to which, if you can keep your body language calm, you have presented an honest face to the viewers!

A really sharp interviewer may spot that you have told only half the truth and still press for the whole story. If the circumstances permit, the best way of disarming this sort of attack is honesty. It is invincible, and you can usually select a safe strand of argument within your case and stick to it.

## Remember this

✳ The skills required are similar to those used in a tough business negotiation.

✳ The secret is to be able to remember and apply the skills in this completely different environment.

✳ This is a world in which your interviewer is completely at home. It is essential to remember that it is you who are the expert in your own subject.

### BODY LANGUAGE IN TELEVISION INTERVIEWS

Most television interviews are not battles, but nevertheless most journalists will play the devil's advocate to give an interview more bite. It is well-known that bad news travels faster than good and that it will make more headlines. The interviewer's role is to prosecute the public case and ask the questions that viewers would like answers to.

The main thing to bear in mind with respect to television interviews is that most people watch television with probably no more than 70 per cent of their attention. Many are doing other things while viewing: preparing a meal, doing the ironing, reading the paper. Even if they are immersed in a favourite programme, their attention might be distracted by the phone ringing or somebody starting a conversation.

This is why body language in television interviews is so crucial. Viewers will generally receive a stronger impression from it than from your words. So it is essential to look comfortable, but to sit up and not slouch – you want to look as though you have authority, not like a sack of potatoes. If you are wearing a jacket, it is a good idea to sit on the tail so that your collar doesn't ride up. Hands should be relaxed; clasp them lightly in your lap if you are sitting down for an interview. Legs can be crossed, but preferably at the ankles. If a man crosses his legs, he should make sure that no distracting stretch of white flesh shows between his socks and the bottom of his trousers. Women should avoid skirts with a tendency to ride up when they are sitting down, as these also distract the viewer's attention from what is being said.

Try to ignore the camera and concentrate on the interviewer and on the questions they are asking. It is seldom that you will actually look into the camera lens unless you are doing a piece 'down the line', which means you are in a remote studio talking to a presenter via a link. In this case, you should look straight at the camera, as it gives the viewer the impression that you are looking the interviewer in the eye. You don't usually have long to make your point in a news interview so you must be thoroughly prepared and have in your mind about three points that you want to get across.

You can tell whether an interview is going well simply by the way the protagonists are sitting.

### Try it now

❋ Turn the television volume to mute.
❋ Look at the way the interviewer is sitting.
❋ Look at the interviewee – is he/she leaning forward or back?
❋ Try to guess how the interview is going.
❋ Now turn the sound back on and see if you were reading the body language correctly.

Do not wear a suit or jacket with a houndstooth-type check or very thin stripes, as these can make the cameras 'strobe'. The same applies to shirts and ties. Colours cause fewer problems nowadays, although it is still better to avoid blocks of white or red. Think about the image you want to project; darker colours are seen as more professional but bright colours will attract the viewer's attention. It is also important to dress appropriately. If the interview is serious, it is better to wear sober colours, whereas if you have won the lottery, why not tell the world how happy you are by wearing something bright and cheerful!

## Key idea

Preparation is the Key to Confidence and Confidence is the Key to Success.

You are likely to be fitted with a microphone. This will pick up even the slightest sound, such as the movement of your clothing, so keep your body relaxed and don't fidget. The monitor television set in the studio will probably distract you when your own picture appears on it. Shifty sideways glances at your image should be avoided – they are lethal to giving an impressive appearance, and people have been known to 'dry' completely as they watch their own performance live! At best, the viewer doesn't know what you are looking at and may conclude that for some reason you are unwilling to look the interviewer in the eye. Equally, don't look directly into the camera. The director or reporter has chosen the camera angles, so let the camera look at you. You look at the interviewer and nowhere else. A good interview should be an interesting conversation that is eavesdropped on by cameras and microphones.

You may have make-up applied before a television interview but this is not always the case. If you are not being made up, men need to have shaved and brushed their hair. Women also need to check their appearance, especially lipstick (make sure there is none on your teeth), and that their hair is tidy. I would also suggest that both men and women add a little face powder, as a shiny face can make it appear that you are nervous, and wearing foundation can counteract the tendency of high-definition cameras to show up every line or blemish.

Finally, relax. Although it is hard in the unfamiliar circumstances and in the knowledge that you are going to be questioned in front of thousands of people, including your colleagues, it is essential that you appear composed and in control.

**Remember this**

✻ You've done your preparation.
✻ You have followed all these hints.
✻ You are more expert than the interviewer about your subject.
✻ Take a series of deep calming breaths – relax.
✻ It is the interviewer's job to keep things going, not yours.

**BODY LANGUAGE IN RADIO INTERVIEWS**
Radio is a less intimidating medium but many of the same rules apply as for television interviews:

▶ make time for adequate preparation

▶ decide the points you want to make.

For radio interviews, it is your voice that is important, and it is essential that you get to know your voice well; Chapter 7 will help you with this. Most people listen to the radio when driving or have it on in the background while doing other things, so it is only your voice that will make listeners sit up and take notice. Your voice must be full of energy, even if the interview is something of an interrogation, and you should seem keen to answer the questions, however searching they are.

Some people think that it doesn't matter how you dress for a radio interview, but that is not the case. The presenter will take you at face value. For instance, if you are invited onto a breakfast show to talk about your book on image, it is important that you look the part so that the interviewer has some belief in the message you are promoting. If you turn up looking as though you have just got out of bed, the interview might go in a very different direction. Also, remember that there is a webcam hovering in the corner of nearly every radio studio these days!

# Press interviews

If a reporter calls you unexpectedly on a subject about which you feel uncertain, don't blurt out the first thing that comes into your head. Offer to make some enquiries and call the reporter back. Then consult someone, or decide for yourself what needs to be said. If you are likely to attract press attention, perhaps because your organization is under attack, try to anticipate what you are likely to be asked and mentally prepare your response.

Remember that the press, unlike radio and television, will probably interrogate you without prior warning. Because the first contact is likely to be over the phone, the tone of your voice is crucial. If you sound wary, it will make a smart reporter even keener to dig for hidden skeletons, so try to keep the tone of your voice light and sound as if you are happy to talk.

Newspaper reporters, especially on the national tabloid papers, are highly paid professionals. Their skills are not literary but investigative, and experienced reporters are skilled in the art of interrogation. Questioning that appears to be both friendly and innocuous may be leading you into a trap, so think hard before you speak. If you are involved in a major news story, reporters will not hesitate to besiege your home or your workplace around the clock, or to call at three in the morning in the hope that you might say something unguarded when struggling out of sleep.

During a face-to-face interview it is important that you look relaxed. Good reporters are expert at reading body language and may interpret a tapping foot or shifting eye contact as a sign that you are hiding something. If the interview is taking place in your office, clear your desk so that you have nothing to distract you. Also, for a telephone interview, try to sit facing a blank wall rather than where you can see out of the window. You need all your concentration to listen carefully to the questions.

Again, how you look and what you wear is significant. Make sure you wear something that projects the image you want to project, and also choose carefully the location where you 'chat' to the journalist. Don't forget your surroundings will be noted and may be used to colour a story. If you are a company director being interviewed about your company making redundancies and you sit with the reporter in your garden next to the swimming pool, you may find the slant of the story weighted against you!

The reporter may employ the notebook ploy. Questions will be asked without any appearance of notes being taken. At some point, the notebook may be ostentatiously put away. Be careful; the notebook (or the mobile phone or tape recorder) may have gone but the interview continues. Because they know that people are inhibited by having notes taken in front of them, reporters, like police officers, train themselves to make a mental note of what is said and then transcribe it into the notebook, or more likely into their phone, after the interview. The rule about talking 'off the record' is simple; don't do it, unless it is someone you know well and trust.

Very often, the reporter already has the story from other sources and you are being approached merely for a quote, a reaction to what has happened. This means that the story will not disappear if you decide not to speak to the press; if your organization is in trouble, an interview can offer an opportunity for damage limitation.

The tabloids specialize in what are called 'human interest' stories, that is stories about people. Generally speaking, the tabloids do not 'make things up'. However, they do tend to simplify, exaggerate or dramatize the stories they cover, because the function of the popular press is to entertain. It is no more sinister than that. It would be a mistake to avoid the press because you believe they are attempting to destroy you or your organization. The press can be very good source of PR for you, so it is worth getting to know your local journalists. Local newspapers are so short-staffed nowadays that many reporters are only too glad to receive well-written copy that saves them time and fills a space, provided that it is relevant, topical and not a blatant advertisement.

### Remember this

* Do not be caught 'on the hop'. Say you will call the journalist back to give yourself time to think.
* Check the journalist's credentials.
* Keep the interview short and make only the statements you have prepared.
* Listen very carefully to the questions.

# Staying within the law

There is one situation in which you must never comment, and that is when the matter under discussion is the subject of criminal proceedings. If someone has been charged with a criminal offence, the matter becomes *sub judice*. This means it cannot be commented on outside the confines of the court without the person making the comment incurring the risk of proceedings for contempt of court. This offence can be punished with a prison sentence.

## Answers to self-assessment

1 So that you look authoritative
2 At the interviewer
3 A conversation
4 No
5 When something is *sub judice*
6 Clear your desk and face a blank wall
7 When the reporter puts the notebook down but continues with the interview
8 Because they can create PR and spread your message
9 White or red
10 Informative and critical

## Focus points

The main points to remember from this chapter are:
❊ prepare thoroughly
❊ get to know your voice
❊ think before you speak
❊ never speak 'off the record'
❊ get to know your local press

## Next step

**Chapter 11 will guide you through the body language of the minefield that is dating. It will show you what signs to look for when trying to work out whether your date finds you attractive, and what you can do to build a successful relationship.**

# 11

# Body language when dating

In this chapter you will learn about:

▶ *personal space*
▶ *bonding signs*
▶ *barrier signals*
▶ *body language when dating men*
▶ *body language when dating women*
▶ *building confidence when dating*
▶ *the first date*
▶ *internet dating.*

## Self-assessment

1 What is a barrier position?

2 How can you make yourself more interesting?

3 Name a sign that shows a man is attracted to a woman.

4 What is a classic signal that shows a woman is attracted to a man?

5 How can you build confidence when dating?

6 What are the signs a couple has built rapport?

7 What are the three 'bubbles'?

8 Why do we 'mirror' each other?

9 What constitutes having good manners?

10 What should you be aware of when internet dating?

Answers are at the end of this chapter.

## Key idea

'Sometimes I wonder if men and women really suit each other. Perhaps they should live next door and just visit now and then.'

Katharine Hepburn

Judging by the number of relationships that fail or break down, Katharine Hepburn's idea might be a good one for some people. But finding a mate has been a fundamental instinct since we evolved on this earth. Men and women *are* different – and *vive la différence*, I say!

For any relationship to work, it needs to include the essential ingredients of respect and good manners. Misunderstandings can often be misinterpreted as bad manners, so it is important to get the communication right. Good manners are ageless, classless and priceless, and everybody should have them. But what are manners today, and do they matter?

## Key idea

'The hardest job kids face today is learning good manners without seeing any.'

Fred Astaire

People with good manners treat others with civility, think of others before themselves and have respect for others, so they tend to make good companions. Having good manners means behaving in a way that is socially acceptable, which is important if your date is to mix happily with your friends. If we all followed the guidelines of good manners and mutual respect, we would treat each other more kindly, behave more honestly and enjoy better relationships.

# Personal space

We all like our own space, and there are roughly three zones or 'bubbles' in which we feel comfortable and make our own:

▶ the intimate bubble

▶ the personal bubble

▶ the public bubble.

The intimate bubble is one to which you will admit only close family members or lovers. In this bubble you will allow intimate contact, particularly round the face, hair, shoulders, arms and legs as well as allowing someone to hold their body against yours. You will permit even more intimate contact where lovers or children are concerned.

The personal bubble encompasses friends and some colleagues. You will be happy for them to put their arm round your shoulder, hold your hand or touch your face or hair briefly. This bubble extends roughly to the length of the arm for most people.

The public bubble is by far the biggest bubble because we all value our space. For most Westerners it extends to at least the length of two arms.

If you are waiting for a train or to see a doctor, you are very unlikely to go and sit next to someone you don't know if there are other seats available. Studies have shown that people tend to leave two seats between themselves and another person if possible. The exception is on commuter trains and subway or Tube trains. In most cities these are nearly always crowded at rush hour, so there is no choice but to be closely packed together. But study the body language. Most travellers look at the ground or the ceiling and seldom look at fellow passengers, let alone smile at them! It is the same in a lift or elevator. Men may try to take a surreptitious look at a woman if there is a mirror handy, or if she is standing sideways on, but women will look steadfastly at the ceiling, their shoes (or someone else's) or at those riveting numbers telling you which floor you are at. The ice will only be broken if there is a sudden mechanical jolt or perhaps a baby or dog joins the group, when women in particular will start a conversation or at least smile in appreciation of the darling baby or the cute puppy. As a human, you like your space because it enables you to sum up another person. In primeval times this was vital to determine whether they were friend or foe and whether you had to be ready for a fight or for flight.

## Bonding signs

When people are developing a rapport with someone, they will start to mirror that person's behaviour. This happens between friends of the same or the opposite sex, but it is especially important in dating as it is a sure sign that you are bonding.

So what is mirroring? You automatically want to get 'in sync' with someone you find attractive, so when that person moves in a certain way, you will do the same. You will find that when the person you are bonding with moves forward, you will unconsciously move forward; when they move back, you will find you are moving back at the same time. If you are having a drink you will often sip your drinks at the same time.

Dilation of the pupils is another sign someone is interested in you, because pupils dilate with excitement. Some professional poker players wear dark glasses so that fellow players can't see their eyes. As you talk to your date, try gazing into their eyes and see if you can detect changes in the size of the pupils.

Playing with a wine glass when having a meal can also be revealing. If your date starts to stroke the stem, it can be a subconscious act telling you what they might be thinking about or imagining. The same applies to stroking a pen, and this can happen in a one-to-one business meeting, never mind on a date! Men will also stroke their ties absentmindedly – these gestures all mean that they are thinking about sex! It is said that men think about sex every 7–10 seconds. Few men will admit to this – and if it were the case, nothing would ever get done! But men do think about sex more often than most women, as they are pre-programmed to procreate as much and as often as possible. In the animal world, males will mate at any time, whereas females will mate only a few times a year.

### Try it now

* Look at the people around you.
* Analyse their body language.
* Study their movements.
* Try to guess whether they are in rapport.

Much of our social behaviour is established from childhood. Girls tend to play in small groups or with one particular friend, whereas boys play in larger groups. Boys' games are more concerned with status and they tend to find natural leaders who organize the rest of 'the gang'. Girls who show the same tendencies are accused of being bossy, and are taught to stand back and let others take a turn.

## Barrier signals

There are several obvious barrier signals. Two of them are manoeuvring backwards from someone or turning the head away. Feet also play an important role in showing where someone wants to be; as mentioned in earlier chapters, look at someone's feet and they will tell you where their attention lies. A classic barrier signal is for someone to have their arms across their chest, although it can mean the person is cold or prefers to stand or sit that way, so it is essential to look at the overall body language to gauge the exact meaning.

Some body language experts call a number of different signals a 'cluster', but I think it is easier to look at the overall picture. If the person looks relaxed and is reacting appropriately to what you are saying, they are not using a position such as crossed arms as a barrier. If, however, they are not making eye contact and keep looking away, it is possible that they are nervous and the crossed arms are protecting a vulnerable part of the body. So it is vital to look at the person's body language as a whole and to take note of your gut feelings. Your intuitive feelings or your 'inner voice' is more than likely to be correct as they arise from a combination of conscious and subconscious signals and chemistry.

We send out different smells and signals that we are unaware of, but which animals can certainly receive and decode. My Jack Russell terrier, Hattie, knows my moods almost before I know them myself! When I was writing this book, if I sighed because I was trying to find the right word, for instance, she came to my chair and looked at me with anxious eyes as she knew I was worried about something. She could smell the change of chemistry as I searched my mind to find the exact word or phrase I wanted. I wasn't really anxious, but Hattie knew I was struggling slightly. On the other hand, when I sighed because I had finished a chapter, she could sense my elation and rushed up with one of her toys for us to play with. Even though humans have lost the ability to read overtly the changes in our temperature or smell, we should not underestimate the subconscious effect these changes can have on each another. So, anxiety can be a barrier signal because it can turn someone off without you even knowing it.

If you are talking to someone at a party and their shoulders are not face on to yours, it is a sign that they would rather be somewhere else. The mouth may smile and the eyes look into yours but if they will not face you, you have a problem! It is important to interpret these signals early so that you don't waste time pursuing something that is going nowhere.

## Body language when dating men

Although it is said that women, especially Western women, dress to impress other women, most women who are dating will do their best to dress and behave in a way that they think men will find attractive.

### Key idea

'Can you imagine a world without men? No crime and lots of happy fat women.'

Marion Smith

It is odd that women should be so concerned about their size, because many men like women who carry a bit of weight, and in some cultures it is seen as a positive sign of beauty, indicating that the family has plenty to eat or that the woman has good child-bearing ability.

In the developed world the differences between men and women in activities, dress and behaviour have decreased over recent decades. Although women have always done men's jobs, they have never before had the equality enjoyed today, and this has had a huge effect on the way people date as women no longer need to rely on a man to pay for them. One thing that hasn't changed, though, is that men like to be appreciated. That may sound obvious – we all like to be appreciated – but men like to know that they are appreciated, so it is important for women to tell them. Never assume someone knows what you mean or think, so when you are asked out for a drink or dinner, compliment your date on his choice of bar or restaurant.

Very often body language will show in what men say. A man will talk about himself and his achievements thinking that this will impress his date. He may expound his views and hold forth in an effort to make himself more interesting. This can have the effect of turning a woman off, as it can make him appear conceited or intractable, but if he is initiating eye contact and looking at his date when he talks, this is a sign that he is trying to impress rather than show off. While it is a good thing to encourage him to talk by maintaining eye contact and nodding in agreement, it can become a rather one-sided conversation for his date! So, it is important for a woman to contribute to the conversation by asking relevant questions and giving her views. This allows the couple to get to know each other gradually and explore each other's likes and dislikes.

## Remember this

Watch out for specific signs when having a drink or a meal:

* stroking his tie
* loosening his collar
* taking off his glasses and playing with the arms
* caressing a wine glass (moving it backwards and forwards or fondling the stem)
* keeping eye contact while resting his chin on his hands (with elbows on the table).

Women should never forget that, genetically, man is a hunter and still enjoys the thrill of the chase, so for a woman to give in too easily or too soon will make him lose interest. It is crucial that a woman doesn't seem too interested in a 'relationship' when she goes on the first few dates, as this is a definite turn-off for most men. Therefore, look at the first date as a chance to see if this man might be worth getting to know further. Indirect compliments can help bring out the best in a man.

**Remember this**

Compliments for men:
* This is a really nice restaurant.
* That was a very good film.
* This picnic was a great idea.
* The music in this club is fantastic.

### BEING ASSERTIVE

There is a big difference between assertiveness and aggressiveness. Assertiveness means standing up for and stating your own opinions and beliefs without putting down anyone else's. Some women feel they have to be aggressive to make a man respect them, but this could not be further from the truth, as it tends to undermine a man's confidence in his ability to please or satisfy a woman. Some women, when nervous or outside their comfort zone, become slightly aggressive, especially if they are in a senior managerial position at work and used to taking control. If you are a working woman who is earning more than her date, you should be careful not to pull the rug from under his feet. The recent changes in the job market have taken place relatively quickly and some older men have not yet come to terms with the fact that their partner might be earning more than they do.

Assertiveness helps you to become more confident about yourself and with others. Everyone has a right to an opinion, and it is important to state yours clearly and to explain why you hold it. Men tend to be more logical rather than emotional in the way they think, so a woman's statement of her opinions or beliefs will be communicated more clearly to the man she is dating if she 'mirrors' the male way of thinking, i.e. giving explanations that are not based purely on emotions or feelings but on a more rational and, if possible, researched approach.

**Remember this**

We need to use empathy as well as assertiveness in our interactions to accomplish successful communication.

✳ 'This is how I see the situation...'

✳ 'This is what I believe and why...'

✳ 'This is what I want and why...'

✳ Say it with a smile.

The choice of 'I' or 'we' can have a significant effect on whether someone sounds confident and creates a positive image. Women tend to use 'we' and to apologize more, but when they say 'I'm sorry', it is often a way of expressing concern rather than an apology. People who don't take credit for what they do or who are constantly apologizing may appear weaker and less confident than they actually are. Men apologize far less, on the whole. Women also pay more compliments than men. If you ask a male colleague what he thought of your outfit the last time you went on a date, don't be surprised if you get an honest answer – if he noticed at all!

# Body language when dating women

A legacy of our primeval past is that women subconsciously look for someone to procreate with who is fit and healthy in order to ensure the longevity of the species. Although we are probably not aware of that instinct these days, a man who looks pallid, overweight and generally unfit is still a turn-off; it would have meant that the prey he needed to catch for the family dinner would most likely have outrun him! So, as I've said before, keeping fit is a good idea.

If a woman fancies a man, there are several tell-tale signs to look out for. Women usually have to be more overt in signalling their interest because many men don't pick up the signs as readily as a woman would. If your date has beautiful hair, she will toss her head to make sure you notice it. She will also play with strands of hair or curls to draw your attention to her hair. Stroking her neck or playing with a necklace is another sign that she wants you to notice her good points.

When women are aroused, their lips engorge with blood; one of the reasons women have reddened their lips for centuries is to look younger and more fertile. Kissing is an integral part of dating, but why do we do it? Anthropologists say it is because in primeval times we were fed by our mothers mouth to mouth after she had masticated the food, the only way food could be made digestible for an infant. You see birds and some animals feeding their young this way. We certainly put things into our mouths or bite our nails as a form of comfort that goes back to the breast or bottle. So if a woman draws attention to her mouth by slowly licking her lips, it usually means she finds the man attractive. If she licks her lips quickly, it often means she is nervous or anxious.

If a couple is sitting at a table and the woman is attracted to the man, she will often rub one foot against her calf, or dangle a shoe off her foot. This again indicates that she wants to get closer to the man and is thinking of more intimate contact.

## Remember this

Watch out for specific signs when on a date:
* fiddling with her hair
* tossing her head
* stroking her neck
* playing with her jewellery
* licking her lips
* rubbing her foot against her calf
* dangling a shoe off her foot.

Some women will say that a sense of humour is one of the most sexy qualities in a man. If you have a good sense of humour, make sure it is acceptable for female company because although some women find 'dirty' or sexist jokes funny, others don't!

## Try it now

* Stand in front of a mirror.
* Look at yourself analytically.
* Do you look fit and healthy?

**Remember this**

Compliments for women:

* You look lovely tonight.
* You certainly know how to choose a good film.
* That colour makes you sparkle.
* You are a brilliant dancer.

# Building confidence

Everybody lacks confidence at some time in their lives. Even the most assured people can feel unsure of themselves and their abilities at some point. Lack of confidence can affect your domestic and work life: a boss who constantly checks everything you do undermines your confidence; a woman who is constantly put down by her husband or partner often lacks self-esteem; teenagers are usually filled with anxiety.

**Key idea**

'Nobody can make you feel inferior without your consent.'

Eleanor Roosevelt

There are many ways to become confident but among the most important are facing your fears, gaining self-knowledge and thinking positive thoughts.

**Try it now**

* Have you always lacked confidence?
* When did you begin to lose it?
* Examine the reasons why it is lacking.
* Look for ways of regaining it.

If you aren't confident, you have a fear for a specific reason. It may be that you fear you may be laughed at if you give your opinions. You may worry about your looks, or be apprehensive that you are not as good as someone else at a specific task. Whatever your anxieties, facing up to them is vital.

**Key idea**

'People would worry less about what others thought about them if they realized how seldom they do.'

Olin Miller

Make a list of all your good points and really appreciate the very special person you are. Everybody has their unique points, so examine what yours are and don't put yourself down. You have as much to offer as the next person, and if you are kind, considerate and make the best of yourself, you will be a great companion for any date!

## The first date

When you first go out with someone you will probably have little idea of their likes, dislikes, interests or hobbies; and they will have little idea about yours. If you feel that you have little in your life apart from work, and so little to talk about, be prepared! Improve your knowledge. There is a wide variety of courses on offer at most local colleges. You might enjoy learning another language, improving your culinary skills, painting, pottery, choral singing, learning a new sport – the possibilities are endless. The other people on a course can often be very interesting, and sharing a class may lead to a date. It is also a way to widen your circle of friends as well as giving you something to talk about! Try also to read a newspaper every day (especially one of the broadsheets) and keep yourself abreast of events, so that you will be able to join in conversations about current affairs.

Who pays if you go out for drinks or dinner? I am old-fashioned enough to expect the man to ask the woman out, and that he should pay on the first date. However, in these days of equality you may prefer to split the bill. This is a good idea if one or both parties don't want to take things further, as it avoids either feeling that they have been used as a meal ticket.

If another date is planned, watch the body language when you are deciding what to do. If you say that you would like to go to the theatre or a football match, see how enthusiastic the response is. If the voice says 'yes' but the body hangs back, it probably means that your date is willing to humour you but that it is not really their idea of a good time. If the voice says 'yes' and the body moves forward, it is likely that they too will look forward to the event.

How intimate should you get? Obviously, this depends on the circumstances, age or desires of the couple involved and is nobody else's business; however, my advice would be to save something for the next date! Read the body language, don't be pushy, and respect each other's wishes.

## Internet dating

Many people have found long-lasting, happy relationships via the internet, but many have also been disappointed when the reality didn't meet expectations. Honesty is the best policy.

### Key idea

'The rarest thing in the world is a woman who is pleased with photographs of herself.'

Elizabeth Metcalf

Elizabeth Metcalf's remark is almost always true, so let a trusted friend choose a photograph of you for your online profile. However much you like a particular picture, if it was taken over five years ago or if it doesn't look like you now because you've changed your hairstyle or put on weight, then don't use it. Use an up-to-date photo that shows you as you are now, but also shows you at your best. A misleading photograph gets a relationship off to a shaky start owing to a basic lack of trust. Using an old picture may get you dates, but if meeting the real you is a let-down, the date might not go any further! When you first meet someone the body language is vital.

By the time you meet someone that you have got to know online, you will probably have exchanged a number of emails and possibly also spoken on the phone. From these contacts you will have formed a mental picture of your date and will think that you know them to a certain extent. If you are wise, you will find out something about their interests so that you have something substantial to chat about.

Internet dating is, however, a contrived form of dating so be aware that slightly extreme body language might be displayed. There could be a variety of reasons for this. Perhaps one of the people isn't quite as young as he or she pretended to be, so they try to inject too much energy into the conversation and use unnatural gestures. Or someone could be disappointed in their date and be over-friendly in an attempt to soften the blow of dumping the prospective partner. So don't make up your mind too fast, but be prepared to listen to your inner voice.

Men and women should make sure their clothes match their age. However good your legs, wearing a very short skirt when over a certain age can look inappropriate. Long, flowing locks and even a lithe figure can be a disappointment if the face doesn't match. Tottering along on overly high heels looks sad at any age, as the body language shows you are fashionable but not comfortable. Whatever age you are, walking energetically and standing up straight will take off more years than wearing something better suited to someone half your age.

### Remember this

* Post a recent photo.
* Don't build up your hopes.
* Be prepared for slightly extreme body language.
* Trust your gut feeling.

## Answers to the self-assessment

1 When someone turns their head away when talking to you
2 Improve your knowledge base
3 Stroking his tie; loosening his collar; taking off and playing with his glasses; caressing his wine glass; keeping eye contact while resting his chin on his hand
4 Playing with a necklace
5 Remember your unique points
6 They start to do things 'in sync'
7 Intimate, personal and public
8 To build rapport
9 Kindness, consideration and respect
10 That someone's body language might be extreme

## Focus points

The main points to remember from this chapter are:

✳ listen to your inner voice
✳ both sexes should have good manners
✳ be realistic about internet dates
✳ *vive la différence!*

## Next step

**Chapter 12 considers social and corporate entertaining. As well as looking at body language when dining or holding a party, it includes advice on what to wear when going to a variety of different events, from black tie dos to barbecues. This will give you the ammunition you need to be confident in any social situation so that your body language will never let you down.**

# 12

# Entertaining and social events

In this chapter you will learn about:

- ► *corporate and social image*
- ► *greeting guests*
- ► *confident eating*
- ► *confident drinking*
- ► *conversation topics to avoid*
- ► *doing a deal over dinner*
- ► *what to wear and when*
- ► *non-verbal signals to be aware of.*

**Self-assessment**

1 How do you greet someone?

2 How can you tell when someone is bored?

3 Where on the plate should salt be poured?

4 What topics of conversation should you avoid over lunch or dinner?

5 Why is wearing the right clothes crucial?

6 What should men wear for Royal Ascot?

7 Why are good table manners important?

8 Which side of the place setting does the pudding spoon go?

9 When should you 'rescue' a woman?

10 Name two things you can eat with your fingers.

Answers are at the end of this chapter.

# Corporate and social image

People put us into categories when they find out what we do for a living. A woman who dresses in a conservative manner and says she is an accountant takes nobody by surprise. If, however, she wears a revealing evening gown and dances till dawn, people might look at her in a different light! The image we portray socially is often different from the image we have at work. You can probably think of teachers who, when you met them after you had left school, seemed totally unlike the person you remembered in the classroom.

The image you create in the workplace should carry over into social occasions in certain circumstances; if you are 'the boss', you can't afford to let your hair down completely at the office party. Similarly, the chief executive of a major corporation should be aware that company shareholders might be present at the same occasion or using the same restaurant or bar, and must make sure that drink never loosens the tongue. Our social and professional body language should match as nearly as possible. An image should be a positive thing that will help you succeed.

But remember, an image has to be maintained once you have taken the trouble to build it up. Don't undo months of good work for the sake of that extra glass of bubbly at the office party or your best friend's wedding.

## Greeting guests

A good host or hostess makes guests feel welcome. Your body language should show warmth through your smile and the tone of your voice when you greet them. The correct greeting is 'How do you do'. This is a statement, not a question, and the answer is 'How do you do'. If you find this rather formal, then 'Good morning/afternoon/evening' is fine, or even just 'Hello'. This should be coupled with a handshake, if appropriate, or a nod of the head; it is not considered correct etiquette in Britain or the USA to kiss on first meeting someone. It is also important if somebody introduces someone else as their 'partner' to establish whether theirs is a business partnership or a personal relationship; a mix-up about this can lead to some unfortunate misconceptions!

It is still the case when making introductions that a man should be introduced to a woman, and younger people to their elders; those elders should be addressed formally unless they invite someone to use their personal name.

When introducing people, especially if you are the host, it is a good idea to include a snippet of information to provide a way into conversation for them. For instance, 'Linda, this is Jamie. Linda has just moved into the area and likes to play golf. Jamie, you're a member of the golf club, aren't you?' They can start talking about golf and then move on to more general topics. It is always best to introduce people even if you find out that they already know each other. If you are not sure whether they have met, then saying 'Harry, I think you know Ben Taylor?' is a way of introducing them whether they are already acquainted or not. As mentioned earlier, it is a good idea to repeat a name, for instance 'How do you do, Ben', to fix it in your mind. Your body language can give you away if you are struggling to remember a name. If you do forget, then apologize and admit it;

this is far better than going through an entire evening unable to use someone's name!

## Remember this

* Younger people should be introduced to their elders, and elders should be addressed formally.
* A man is introduced to a woman.
* Don't kiss on first meeting.
* Repeat someone's name when you are introduced to them.

# Confident eating

Raucous laughter, talking with food in your mouth and stretching across the table is body language to be avoided at mealtimes! When you are called to the table, whether in a restaurant or a private house, don't wait to finish your drink or continue a fascinating conversation. Whoever has prepared the food will not be pleased to see it spoil or go cold. If nobody else makes a move, stand up and head quietly for the table. At a formal meal guests should not take their drinks to the table with them; and it is rude to gulp a drink down before going to the table – it looks as if you aren't sure whether you will get another! – so leave what remains in the glass. On less formal occasions your host will usually suggest that you take the glass with you, and a waiter will take drinks to the table in a restaurant.

Guests should wait to be seated by their host or hostess, but if guests are told to sit anywhere, it is usual for spouses or partners to separate, and to alternate male and female guests around the table. Women sit first, but hesitate a moment before taking your seat in case grace is going to be said or any other ceremony observed. It used to be customary for the man to pull back the chair of the woman on his right, but it is rare these days so a woman need not wait for this.

On formal occasions, the most important man sits on his hostess's right, and the next most important on her left. The most important woman sits on the host's right, and the next on his left. This is also the case at single-sex business dinners. At a formal dinner, the host and hostess usually start a conversation first with the person to their right, so follow their lead.

## THE CUTLERY CONUNDRUM

Using the correct implements is an aspect of table manners that worries many people, and getting this wrong, or anxiety about getting it wrong, leads to body language showing someone is extremely uncomfortable. Here are some guidelines to help.

The table is usually laid so that every implement, except the soup spoon and the butter knife, has a partner, but you don't always use every implement. When confronted by a bewildering array of cutlery, a good rule of thumb is to start at the outside and work inwards. However, this rule is not infallible – some people lay the butter knife on the side plate, some above the plate and below the pudding spoon and fork, and others on the left or right of the larger knives – so another rule of thumb is to watch what everyone else does and copy them.

The classic way to set the table for a four-course meal is, working inwards from the right:

► the soup spoon on the outside

► next to it, the butter knife

► then the knife for the main course

► next to it, the pudding spoon

► finally, the cheese knife.

Then on the left, working inwards:

► the fork for the main course on the outside

► next to it, the pudding fork.

Obviously, if the meal has more than four courses, you will have more cutlery. Don't be daunted if you do make a mistake – either carry on eating with confidence or acknowledge the fact that you always get confused and start again.

## Remember this

❋ The 'correct' way to hold a knife is to tuck the handle into the palm of the right hand, with the index finger on top of it, pointing towards the blade; do not hold the knife like a pen.

❋ Hold the fork in a similar fashion, with the handle in the palm of the left hand and the tines pointing towards the plate.

❋ Soup and pudding spoons are held like a pen, but parallel to the table rather than pointing downwards.

❋ When using only a fork, the tines of the fork face upwards, unless you are cutting food. When you are not eating, put the utensils on the plate in an inverted V shape to show that you have not finished. The handles should never rest on the table.

❋ Keep your elbows close to your sides and your hands low.

❋ Lift food up to your mouth rather than dipping your head to meet it.

In Europe it is considered correct to use the knife and fork together, whereas in the USA people cut the food up with both implements and then transfer the fork to the right hand to eat.

On a formal occasion, you will also have a napkin, which should be laid across your lap and not used as a bib. Finger bowls filled with cool water may also be provided; cool water is used because it does not open the pores, which would allow odours to penetrate the skin.

### PECULIAR PRACTICES

The 'rules' above do not apply in certain cases, however, when implements may be used differently or not at all – there are some foods that it is 'correct' to eat with your fingers.

▶ Canapés and dips are very popular at both professional and social drinks parties. When encouraged to 'have a little more', one is left in a quandary about whether to follow the rules of basic hygiene or go ahead and dunk again. Follow the 'one dip per chip' rule or else turn the piece of crudité round and dip the unlicked end. Put used cocktail sticks or olive stones onto an empty plate or, if there is nowhere else available, in your pocket.

▶ In Britain it is considered correct to break bread rolls rather than cut them. To butter the bread, put some butter on the edge of your plate first and then apply butter to a small piece of the broken bread, rather than to the whole piece of bread. It is also polite to spread pâté, cheese or jam the same way.

▶ Salt should be poured, or taken with a spoon, and put at the edge of the plate; even chips should be dipped into the salt and then eaten. Sea salt from a grinder is treated like pepper, which is sprinkled or ground over the food. Mustard, other condiments and sauces should also be placed on the edge of the plate. It is slightly insulting to your host or hostess if you season food before even tasting it, so try a little first.

▶ Rice and pasta should be eaten with a fork, held in the right hand with the tines facing upwards.

▶ Pâté is eaten only with a knife, which is used to spread it on the toast or bread provided.

▶ A savoury soufflé is eaten with a fork, and a sweet soufflé with a spoon.

▶ The correct way to eat soup is push the spoon away from you as you scoop up the soup, and then to sip it from the side of the spoon. In some Far Eastern countries people lift the bowl to the mouth.

▶ Asparagus is eaten with the fingers when served on its own; it is eaten with a knife and fork when served with other vegetables. On its own, the asparagus spear should be held at the fat end and the tips dipped into a sauce, which is poured on to the plate. It's not 'correct' to put a fork under the plate to allow the sauce to gather at one end, which some restaurants do, although it seems ideal to me!

▶ Globe artichokes are also eaten with the fingers. If the middle leaves have been removed, the sauce goes in the hole left in the centre; otherwise it goes on the plate. Pull off the outer leaves, and dip the fleshy end into the sauce, biting hard enough to take off the flesh as you pull the leaf out of your mouth. Put discarded leaves on the plate provided. When you reach the succulent base, eat it with a knife and fork.

▶ Corn on the cob is rolled in butter and then bitten into carefully while holding the cob at each end with the fingers or special holders.

▶ Frogs legs, and spare ribs, are eaten with the fingers.

▶ Snails are held by the shells with special tongs, and the snail twisted out with a sharp, two-pronged fork.

▶ Eat fish off the bone rather than filleting it on the plate. Remove the fine bones with your knife and fork and put them on one side. If you get a fish bone in your mouth, discreetly make a fist with your hand and deposit the bone into it before putting on the side of your plate.

▶ Oysters and mussels can be lifted out of their shells with a fork or you can use a mussel shell as a pair of pincers. During dinner, only the juice of an oyster should be drunk from a shell; otherwise, use a soup spoon to finish any liquid. The empty shells should be put on the plate provided.

▶ If prawns and shrimps are served in their shells, you take off the head with your fingers, lift the shell away from the body and take it off before removing the tail. Once shelled, prawns and shrimps are eaten with a knife and fork.

▶ Crab and lobster are awkward to eat unless the flesh has been dressed and put back into the shells. Larger claws are broken with a cracker and then the meat is scooped out with a lobster pick. For the smaller claws, use the fingers to remove the meat and then eat it with a knife and fork. Brown bread and butter is served to be eaten with crab, not to have the crabmeat spread on it. Both these shellfish can be rather messy to eat, so finger bowls and generously sized napkins are advisable.

▶ Game used to be the only meat that was eaten with the fingers, but now it is customary to use a knife and fork for the sinewy legs unless your host picks up theirs and gnaws it. If they do this, feel free to do the same.

▶ Puddings should be eaten with a spoon and fork, or just a fork, unless served in a glass or small bowl; in this case, use a teaspoon.

▶ On more formal occasions, fruit is halved with a knife and then eaten either with a knife and fork or with the fingers.

▶ Juicy fruit can be a problem, drenching you or your neighbour, so cut or bite into oranges and ripe mangoes carefully!

▶ Cherry stones and grape pips are best dealt with in the same way as fish bones.

▶ Grapes should be cut or pulled off the bunch in small clusters.

▶ Melons and paw-paws are eaten with a spoon or a knife and fork.

▶ Kiwi fruit should be cut in half and then eaten with a teaspoon.

## Confident drinking

A display of glasses can sometimes be a puzzle. There should be as many glasses as the drinks you will be offered. The tallest and slimmest holds champagne, as tulip-shaped glasses are the fashion now. The largest glass is for red wine, and the next down in size holds the white wine; the smaller ones are for sherry (with soup) or port. Incidentally, no wine glass should be filled more than two thirds full (with perhaps the exception of champagne), as it swamps the bouquet. Tumblers are for spirits or water, but water can also be served in a red wine glass. One tip, if you know you are likely to be drinking very good wine, avoid wearing strong perfume or after shave as it will mask the bouquet.

There are many excellent books on the subject of wine. If you are not sure what to order, ask the waiter what he or she would recommend to go with what people are eating. If you are hosting an important event, check the venue beforehand. Even if you are unable to have a meal there before the event, visit the place and talk to the head waiter, and if possible the wine waiter, to discuss menus.

When entertaining at home, go to a good wine merchant and tell them what you are planning to eat. The wine may cost a little more, but it will be worth it. Ideally, give yourself time to try the wines. However highly recommended they are, if you don't like them, don't buy them.

Cocktails have come back into fashion recently, and there is a delicious array of cocktails available nowadays. They are usually much stronger than they taste, so beware! Don't gulp them down, or drain the drink to the last drop when using a straw as you might make an inelegant slurping sound. A good alternative is 'mocktails' (non-alcoholic cocktails) if you are at a business occasion, as it will help you to keep a clear head. Drunken body language is a definite turn off!

## Conversation topics to avoid

It is a good idea to mix different groups when entertaining but try to make sure people have something in common. You can tell when people are in rapport; if they are leaning towards each other and have good eye contact, it is a good sign that they are getting on well with each other. However, there are certain subjects that should be avoided when entertaining.

Religion can be a very private matter for some people and can also be a highly divisive topic. Sex is better kept in the bedroom! To talk about how much money or how many possessions one has is considered crass in most western societies. Talk of illness can make people feel uncomfortable and it is not a topic most people want to hear about when they are eating.

You should be able to see from someone's body language if they are not happy with a topic of conversation. They will move back and sit against the back of the chair or, if standing, lean against a wall. They will turn their head away and often put a hand to their mouth as if to stifle a retort. They might also roll their head to free a build-up of tension in the neck, or purse their lips. They could drum their fingers or fiddle with a watch or jewellery. All this shows that there is resentment or even anger at what is being said, so the subject should be changed as soon as possible.

## Doing a deal over dinner

Business deals are frequently discussed and concluded over lunch or dinner so it is important that the atmosphere is conducive. Most people are not happy sitting with their back to an open door or space – it is a hangover from our primeval past when we were literally protecting our backs from attack – so sit your client with their back to a wall or a screen or some plants; somewhere he or she will feel secure.

Try to do the deal before any food is served. When we have eaten, the blood supply in our bodies is concentrated in our stomachs, as we need it to digest the food, rather than in the brain – which is not good when decisions have to be made! So conclude the business first and then enjoy the social occasion.

Some people will prefer a round table to a square one for business meals because it is less confrontational; I don't think the shape of the table makes any difference when eating a meal. If your table is square and this concerns you, don't sit opposite your client, sit to one side of them.

## What to wear and when

'Know, first, who you are; and then adorn yourself accordingly.'

Epictetus

Another source of social anxiety for many people is whether they are dressed correctly for the occasion. Feeling that you are not appropriately dressed affects your body language – there is more on this later in the chapter, but first here are some guidelines.

## INVITATION DRESS CODES

If an occasion is described as 'black tie', it means that men should wear a dinner jacket which is black with a roll collar and satin-faced lapels, trousers with satin stripes down the outer seams of the trousers and a black bow tie. For women, this dress code means a long evening dress, if attending a dance, or a short cocktail dress or evening trousers for drinks or dinner.

Originally when an invitation stated 'informal', it meant that men did not need to wear morning dress (i.e. a jacket with tails) or medals; nowadays it means that men should wear a smart suit and women smart day wear. If the dress code is 'casual', it can mean anything from jeans to shorts – for something like a barbecue either would be suitable.

If you are unsure what would be suitable for the occasion, check with your host.

## HORSE RACING

Flat racing takes place in the summer, the Derby and Royal Ascot meetings being the most socially prestigious, and dressy, occasions. If you are not in the Royal Enclosure at Ascot, men should wear a smart suit and women a smart day dress and coat or summer suit. In the Royal Enclosure, men should were grey morning dress. Women's skirts must not be too short, and sundresses should be avoided. Stockings or tights should be worn. Most people wear hats at Royal Ascot, but they are only obligatory for the Royal Enclosure. For the Royal Ascot meeting, a slip is usually sent with vouchers for the Royal Enclosure mentioning points of etiquette. One to remember is that mobile phones are not allowed. The dress is similar for other flat race meetings, such as Goodwood, although some, York and Chester for example, are not so formal.

National Hunt racing occurs throughout the year, but predominantly from autumn to spring, and the big social occasions are the Cheltenham Festival and the Grand National. Here, a warm winter suit of fairly muted colours is most suitable, with a warm coat (as the weather is usually cold) and a hat; many women like to wear a trilby. For a more casual approach, jackets and skirts fit the bill. If you are not in a box, a Barbour or waxed jacket and warm trousers will be fine. Boots or stout shoes are also needed as the ground can be soggy.

Point-to-point races are run by horses who have hunted and the riders are usually amateurs. These are much more casual affairs. The season runs from the end of February to late April, so a warm jacket with a skirt or trousers, green Hunter wellies and a Barbour will keep you warm and dry. A trilby hat or a cap is also a good idea for extra warmth, as well as an umbrella.

## SHOOTING AND FISHING

You are unlikely to be asked game shooting unless you have shot before, and most women only accompany their partners to enjoy a good lunch, unless they are keen to help beat. To tramp the grouse moors you will need a warm shirt, a pullover, gloves and a tweed suit or warm trousers. Colours should be muted to help you blend in to the terrain. Thick socks to go inside wellingtons or shooting boots and a Barbour jacket complete the ensemble. For a clay shoot, a body warmer is usually worn over a jersey, thick skirt or trousers, and walking shoes or boots. A hat or cap is advisable when the weather is cold, as are shooting gloves.

Fishing, especially for salmon, can mean wading waist deep into icy streams, so a pair of waders is a must! A pair of warm trousers or jeans, a warm jersey, a Barbour, gloves and green wellies will be needed if the weather is very cold. Some kind of headgear is advisable both for warmth and safety. A fishing fly in the head can be a nasty experience, even more so in the eye, so glasses are often worn for extra protection.

## GOLF

If you are going to play golf seriously, go to the professionals' shop. When you are buying your clubs, you will be shown a wide range of clothes and shoes suitable for all seasons and at a range of prices.

The only thing to be aware of is that some clubs do not allow jeans, shorts or T-shirts on the golf course, so check with the club or fellow guests before donning your bermuda-length shorts, even in the hottest weather.

## TENNIS

If you are invited to the Centre Court or Number One Court at Wimbledon, bear in mind that cameras are not allowed. Check with your host whether there are specific rules for other such events. Dress depends on the weather. A dress and jacket is the most versatile, as it is suitable for all weathers, but a summer suit that can be worn with a blouse underneath is also apt.

## SAILING

The most important thing when invited to go sailing is to have rubber-soled shoes to give you a good grip on deck. Sailing shops sell various types of deck shoes or wellingtons, depending on the weather. Hospitality sailing is usually a very social affair, with a trained crew on hand to actually sail the boat. Most skippers are happy to show you the ropes if you fancy taking the helm, otherwise gin and tonic or hot rum are the order of the day! Take warm trousers and sweaters as well as gloves and a waterproof jacket if sailing in this country, as it can get very cold at sea.

## HENLEY REGATTA

Skirts must reach the knee if you are invited into the Members' Enclosure. Otherwise, a summer suit or smart day dress is fine. Hats are optional.

## GLYNDEBOURNE OPERA

This is a summer event, and most people take a picnic that is eaten in the gardens outside the opera house if the weather is dry – regardless of the temperature. The usual dress for men is a dinner jacket, but women should check with their hostess whether to wear a short or long evening dress. It is advisable to take an overcoat and an umbrella, as well as a rug to sit on.

## CHELSEA FLOWER SHOW

This usually takes place in late May and it can be a fairly formal occasion if you are enjoying corporate hospitality. A blazer or lightweight suit for men and a summer dress with a jacket for women are always suitable.

# Non-verbal signals to be aware of

I have concentrated so much on clothes in this chapter because of the impact of what you wear on your body language. If you are not dressed appropriately and are uncomfortable, you can appear ill at ease and may transmit negative signals without being aware of it.

Shifting from foot to foot or changing position frequently when sitting are two signs that someone is not comfortable. Ask whether there is anything wrong, but don't press them if they say they are fine; their discomfort might be for personal reasons or because they are not dressed appropriately. This body language can also occur because someone is tired and is shifting to keep themselves awake, or they might want to go to the loo. They will tell you if they need to answer a call of nature! Try to avoid having to leave the table yourself for this reason during a meal, as it disrupts conversation and will leave one person with no one to talk to while you are away.

Other non-verbal signals to be aware of when entertaining are eye contact, or the lack of it, and the position of your guests' feet. If someone is bored by another person, their eye contact will begin to wander or their eyes will glaze over. Glance at the feet in this case, and if these are pointing away from the person they are talking to, they need rescuing! A rescue is also needed if a conversation is very one-sided, and particularly if a woman is being slowly backed into a corner!

If someone is fiddling with rings or 'washing' their hands, they are anxious, perhaps because they feel it is late but they don't know how to make a polite departure. In this case you should ask if anything is wrong or make them feel at ease by saying something like 'Goodness, look at the time!'. This will allow them to tell you they need to go home etc.

Another sign of boredom, or just bad manners, is using a phone during a meal or texting while talking to someone. Phones should be switched off during mealtimes, and to text while talking to someone is the height of bad manners.

If two of your guests run out of conversation during dinner, this will usually show in sporadic speech and a general lack of rapport. They will turn away from each other, or even turn their backs on each other, if they find they have nothing in common or don't like one other. A useful ploy in such situations, and one that livens things up at any time, is to have the male guests move round two places at the table, giving all the guests the chance to talk to someone else. This problem is less likely to arise at cocktail parties or dances because people can move away, but during a meal the body language is more pronounced because they are trapped in their place at the table.

## Answers to the self-assessment

1 By shaking hands and saying 'how do you do'
2 Lack of eye contact
3 Onto the side of the plate
4 Religion, sex, money and illness
5 To ensure positive body language
6 Morning dress
7 It shows sophisticated body language
8 On the right
9 When a woman is being backed into a corner
10 Asparagus (as a first course); globe artichoke; corn on the cob; frog's legs; spare ribs; some fruit (once sliced).

## Focus points

The main points to remember from this chapter are:
* don't use mobile phones during mealtimes or text in company
* don't leave the table during a meal – if desperate to answer a call of nature, wait until after the pudding
* Keep an eye on your guests' body language
* Make sure people are properly introduced to each other
* if in doubt about anything – food, wines, dress, etiquette – ASK!

**Next step**

Chapter 13 considers body language in a worldwide context, as it differs according to the culture in each country or region. There are pitfalls to avoid so that you do not offend anybody when working or holidaying abroad.

# 13

# Different cultures, different rules

In this chapter you will learn:

- ▶ *greetings*
- ▶ *business etiquette*
- ▶ *signals to be aware of*
- ▶ *the dos and don'ts of entertaining*
- ▶ *the dos and don'ts of dress.*

## Self-assessment

1 How should you give a business card to a Japanese businessperson?

2 How do people say 'yes' in Pakistan?

3 What is the greeting in the Middle East?

4 What is namaskar?

5 Where is it rude to blow your nose in public?

6 Where do men hug?

7 What should Western businesspeople learn about when working in Arabic countries?

8 How low is an informal Japanese bow?

9 When do you pay for a meal?

10 What can the OK circle of finger and thumb mean?

Answers are at the end of this chapter.

Body language varies from country to country. This chapter can only skim the surface of this aspect, but should give you some basic guidance on what to do and not to do when you are doing business abroad. Apart from learning a little of the language of the country where you propose to do business, you should also master cultural differences in etiquette and manners. When you work overseas or with people from different backgrounds, doing familiar jobs in unfamiliar circumstances can have a significant effect on business. It is vital to find out as much as you can about the country you are about to visit. Chambers of commerce, trade associations and the embassies of the countries concerned can provide information and guidelines, and are usually very helpful. The internet is also a useful source of information, as well books on the subject.

## Key idea

'It is useful to know something about other nations' habits in order to judge our own in a healthier fashion, and not imagine everything which differs from ours should be dismissed as ridiculous or illogical, as is frequently done by those who haven't seen anything.'

René Descartes

# Greetings

In most cultures, gestures of greeting developed as a means of showing that you were unarmed, such as the handshake using the right hand, or sword arm, in Western society.

In the Middle East, the greeting is the salaam. The full salaam involves curving the right hand upwards with the open palm facing the body, then touching the chest above the heart, before touching forehead with fingers. To finish, the hand sweeps up and out with the palm facing the recipient. Often 'Assalam 'alaikum' ('Peace be with you') is said at the same time. In a shorter version of the salaam, the hand touches the forehead and then sweeps away.

The Malaysian salaam involves extending the hands, putting fingers together and then placing the hands on the chest.

In India, the tradition is to make a namaskar to greet others. Both hands are held up together at chest level, as if praying.

**Try it now**

Stand in front of a mirror.

✳ Practise the salaam.

✳ Make a namaskar.

In Japan, bowing is still prevalent. It is a time-honoured way of saying: 'I accept your wisdom and experience.' There are several different bows, including:

▶ the formal bow – the body is bent forward to about 30–45 degrees, with the hands placed on the knees. A bobbing up and down action follows until the most important person rises first.

▶ the informal bow – the body is bent forward to about 15 degrees, and the hands remain at the side of the body.

Most Japanese people greet each other informally with a bow, but they usually prefer to shake hands with Westerners as we cannot work out the depth or length of the bows!

The Chinese will also shake hands with Westerners, but probably do a lot of hand pumping.

Kissing as a greeting is common in much of Europe and the Americas, but it is frowned upon in Asia. In Britain, people used to kiss just one cheek, and this was reserved for family and very close friends. Nowadays, as global travel becomes more widespread, we have picked up social habits from other cultures. Two, three or even four kisses may be exchanged in France and the Netherlands, and you need your wits about you to work out how many kisses you might expect to receive! Kissing accompanied by a 'mwa, mwa' sound is considered insincere; there is no need to make any noise, just brush your cheek against theirs. Hand-kissing is a charming habit that is little used nowadays, although it is still quite common in Latin America. The kiss may include brushing the hand or not quite making lip contact. In some countries, France and Russia for example, hugging and kissing is a normal form of greeting between men, as is hugging in Latin American countries.

## Remember this

* A brief nod usually means agreement, but a prolonged nod shows doubt, and in parts of India it can mean 'no'.
* Shaking the head in most cultures means 'no', but in India, Pakistan and Bulgaria a 'head wobble' that looks like shaking the head actually means 'yes'.
* In China and some parts of Africa it is deemed respectful to lower the eyes when talking to older or more senior people, so you should do the same.
* In the West when we are introduced to anyone, it is good manners to look them in the eye and smile.

# Business etiquette

In much of Asia, especially Japan, it is important to know the rank of the person you are dealing with; this goes for any business meeting. South-east Asians assess a businessperson by their status and contacts, so make sure you have a good-quality wallet with a large number of impressive business cards in it.

Exchanging business cards is an important part of business etiquette in Asia. Cards should be presented and received with either the right hand or both hands, with the name pointed towards the recipient. It is important to look at the card to acknowledge the importance of the giver, and then the card should be put on the table beside you. Place it in your card wallet at the end of the meeting, never in your back pocket.

In China, the surname comes first and the forename last. Make sure you know which is the surname and use this, as over-familiarity at a first meeting is not considered good etiquette.

### Key idea

If you are a frequent business traveller, make sure you are provided with a list of the key people you will meet, country by country, with their surnames underlined, and memorize these during your flights.

# Signals to be aware of

Some body language signals are positive in certain cultures and negative in others. In Japan it is most impolite to use a handkerchief to blow one's nose in public, so the Japanese will sniff, which Westerners consider rather coarse. So if you are with Japanese people when you feel a sneeze coming, head for somewhere private, such as the toilet. Similarly, spitting is considered ill-mannered in most countries, but the Chinese and Japanese believe that it is better to get rid of mucus from the body.

# The dos and don'ts of entertaining

Although the culture surrounding eating has become more global these days, there are still marked cultural differences. In many societies it is regarded as an insult not to try a national delicacy, so try a little. One tip is to slice everything very thinly and try not to think what it might be or where it has come from. Squeamishness often arises from unfamiliarity rather than the item itself, so if you are offered a sheep's eye, think of it as an oyster and swallow hard! An acquaintance who does a lot of business in China has had experience of several 'banquets' comprising unknown and unappetizing dishes. On a recent visit, when asked which banquet he would like for dinner that night, he plumped for seafood. 'I thought I was safe as I am a bit of an expert on anything to do with the sea, but blow me down if I wasn't presented with some horrible wiggling worms that I had never come across in my life before!'

In China, leaving a little food on your plate is a sign that you have had enough to eat. In Britain, it used to be polite for ladies to leave a morsel or two to show that they had eaten an 'elegant 'suffiency'; nowadays it is considered wasteful to take more than you are going to eat.

In France, business meals may be rather lavish and expensive. Breakfast meetings are popular, and can be held in a café, your hotel or the company's dining room. Although a business lunch can still be a leisurely affair, the days of habitually long lunches are over, and a quick brasserie lunch is the norm for day-to-day dealings. Whoever issues the invitation pays the bill, and business should not be discussed until the coffee stage.

Both Spain and Portugal are very hospitable countries and your contacts will want to pay for you, so let them if they insist. Breakfast meetings are not very common. Lunches and dinners are the norm, and are likely to be drawn-out affairs. In Portugal you are likely to be invited to someone's home, or even away for the weekend; a thank-you letter afterwards is always appreciated.

In the Netherlands and Luxemburg lunch is the most usual form of business entertaining but it is unlikely to be a very ostentatious affair – perhaps only beer and a sandwich – and whoever issues the invitation pays. Dinner is more relaxed, but little business will be discussed as it is seen as a chance to get to know each other better. If you are invited to someone's home, it is a real compliment, so the hosts will appreciate a letter of thanks afterwards. Both these countries tend to be rather formal.

Sweden, Norway, Denmark and Finland tend to be lumped together as 'Scandinavia', but they have very differing cultures and it is important to find out as much as possible about these before you go. Breakfast meetings are popular, where the meal is substantial, but lunch hours are fairly short, so you are most likely to be asked out for dinner. This could be at someone's home or in a restaurant. If you eat at someone's home, it is important to phone and thank them the next day, especially in Denmark.

Accepting an invitation to lunch or dinner is important in Italy, or you might risk appearing uncivil. Whoever issues the invitation usually pays. Bear in mind Italian timekeeping and don't make an appointment too soon after lunch!

Never offer alcohol in Arab countries, but you may accept it if is offered to you.

### Key idea

'If I am selling to you I speak your language; if I am buying ... dann müssen Sie Deutsch sprechen.'

A German politician on a visit to London

### Remember this

* In Hong Kong, the buyer may not get to know you personally or meet you for lunch or dinner until there is a good business reason for doing so.
* In Spain, you will not close a deal unless the client feels he or she knows you well enough to feel they could trust you.
* South-east Asians judge a businessperson by their status and contacts.
* In the USA, the contract is what counts and the written word is all-important.
* In many Middle Eastern cultures, business discussions blend naturally into personal conversation and family life. Deals rely very much on the spoken word and everything is renegotiable between friends.
* If working in Arab countries, Western businesspeople should learn something about Islam, as religion infuses every aspect of life there.

### Key idea

Cultures vary across nations and within nations. No culture is inherently superior or inferior, just different, and you need to be aware of these differences in order to be successful. Getting it wrong can lose you business.

# The dos and don'ts of dress

Dress codes vary in different countries and it is important to be aware of what is proper and respectful. In all Muslim countries women should not wear short skirts or have bare shoulders. Leggings or very tight trousers should also be avoided as they are seen as provocative. Whether or not you agree with these sentiments, it is good manners to respect other cultures and abide by their rules. It is also worth finding out what is meant by 'casual' dress in other cultures. A friend who is an Italian interpreter is often appalled by what some British businessmen wear to go out to dinner. In Italy, 'casual' means smart trousers, good shoes and a quality shirt – not jeans and trainers!

Wherever you travel, what you wear among foreigners should not look foreign to them. This means wearing clothes in which you look natural and feel comfortable but which are also appropriate in your surroundings. Although Western business dress is accepted around the world, when you are 'off duty' and being entertained in the evening, don't imitate, but blend in. For instance a woman wearing a tailored suit in India can look rather masculine in a land of floating saris, so something silky and loose-fitting in bright colours would be suitable. In many hot countries, going tieless and jacketless is often the norm, but take a jacket and tie with you, as some business meetings are formal.

Whether or not to wear shoes can be problematic in the Far East. Shoes are forbidden in mosques and Buddhist temples, and should not be worn in Japanese homes (unless the owner insists otherwise) or some restaurants. In India and Indonesia, if your host is shoeless then you should be too. When you take your shoes off, place them neatly together facing the door you came in by.

I can't stress strongly enough the need to be sensitive to the local culture wherever you go. It is better to be slightly over-dressed than under-dressed; all cultures appreciate it if you have taken time and care, as this shows respect for the people and the country you are visiting.

## Answers to the self-assessment

1 With both hands

2 With a wobble of the head

3 Salaam

4 The greeting in India

5 Japan

6 Russia

7 Islam

8 15 degrees

9 When you give the invitation

10 'Great' in North America and Europe, but worthlessness in some countries.

## Focus points

The main points to remember from this chapter are:

* do your research when visiting another country
* learn a little of the language
* be prepared to try different foods
* dress appropriately
* be aware of different religions.

## Next step

**Chapter 14 looks at body language in tricky situations. Under stress our body language often betrays us, so the chapter provides advice on how to deal with some tricky situations.**

# 14

# Tricky situations

In this chapter you will learn about:

▶ *dealings with the law*
▶ *the driving test*
▶ *making a complaint*
▶ *dealing with the bereaved.*

We all find ourselves in difficult and uncomfortable circumstances at some time in our lives. In tricky or strange situations you will undoubtedly feel under stress and this will show in your body language. As first impressions can have a significant effect on how you are perceived, it is vital to learn to control your conscious and subconscious reactions. The breathing techniques mentioned in earlier chapters will help, as will the following exercise in tensing and relaxing your muscles.

## Try it now

* Sit down quietly.
* Let yourself unwind.
* Take deep, slow breaths.
* Concentrate on your body.
* Tense every muscle.
* Relax each muscle in turn.
* Be aware of each muscle as you begin to relax.

This exercise can be done without anyone noticing and will help to prepare you for most tricky situations.

# Dealings with the law

Our appearance not only makes that all-important first impression, it is often the thing others find particularly memorable about us. Police officers find that clothing is what witnesses to an incident remember most. Black or dark colours are still perceived to be more professional. If a woman is pretty, blonde and wears high heels, she could be seen as an air-head. If a man has long hair, he might be considered unconventional. Someone wearing heavy rimmed glasses might be classified as 'intellectual'. A woman with very short hair and wearing a tie and trousers might have assumptions made about her sexual orientation.

These are very obvious stereotypes, but you should be aware of how your appearance might be perceived if you have to give evidence in court. The jury does not know you, and knowing nothing about you, their initial judgement is going to be based on how you look. The aim is to look as appropriately dressed as possible; otherwise someone might think 'I didn't like that suit', rather than 'That was a very interesting point she/he made'.

Around 20 years ago, at the trial of former American sportsman O. J. Simpson, lawyers started to 'make over' witnesses so that their appearance promoted a positive image and make them more acceptable to juries. Whatever the rights or wrongs of this approach, it shows the power and importance of the image you project and the impression you leave. Creases, tears, holes, stains, loose buttons, frayed collars and cuffs, uneven hemlines or laddered tights all make a negative first impression – so make sure that your clothes do not let you down. Realizing that you are not looking your best will affect your body language and could make you look shifty and consequently lacking in credibility. Sitting up straight rather than lounging in your seat shows confident body language, as does an upright posture when standing. Looking alert and interested in proceedings also makes a positive impression.

When giving evidence of any kind, the voice should be clear and strong; as mentioned in Chapters 3 and 7, you need to listen to your voice and get to know it, so that you can use it effectively to convey your message. If you are giving evidence in court, it is important to be aware of the body language of the judge or magistrate as well as the jury, if there is one. The judge will direct the jury, therefore his or her impression of your body language as well as of what you say will have a direct impact on how the jury will come to a decision. So be aware of the way you sit, how you listen and the expression on your face. You cannot smile if the reason you are in court is a serious one, but to sit with no expression or a constant frown will not send the right signals either. So look interested, but respectful. Arrogance should be avoided at all costs.

Sue Hardy, an independent social worker and an expert witness in child protection cases, finds that watching the body language of the judge is crucial. If the judge starts taking or reading notes, Sue will slow down or pause until she regains his or her attention. Body language also plays a part in how Sue draws up her evidence. 'When I interview families to see who should look after the children, body language plays an essential part. If a parent's eyes light up when they talk about the child, if they have real warmth in the voice, it makes a positive impression,' says Sue. 'The interaction between them and the child or children shows me how close they are and the depth of the bond between them, but it is important to look at the whole picture, not just isolated actions.' Sue recalls interviewing the father in a custody case and his eye contact kept shifting towards the window. Eventually, Sue asked him why he wasn't giving her his full attention – the reason he kept looking out of the window was to make sure her car hadn't been stolen from the street outside!

Sue is very aware of her body language and appearance too. It is normal for her to see several such cases a week, but for anyone going through the traumatic experience of a court case, seeing the social worker, police officer, solicitor or barrister is major event. As a result it is important that people in those professions appreciate how the experience can affect the frame of mind and therefore the body language of those they interview.

# The driving test

Driving tests can be an ordeal for many people. I have friends who are perfectly good drivers but who have failed their test several times simply through nerves and nervous body language. Examiners are looking for confidence and competence. They want to know that you will remain cool in an emergency and not go to pieces; so if you fall apart when asked to do an emergency stop, you will never pass the test! However well you can drive, if you crouch over the steering wheel and grasp it as though it is going to fly out of your hands any minute, you will not give the impression that you are in control of yourself, never mind the car. Being relaxed in mind and body is vital, but how can you achieve this? It is all down to preparation. Learn your Highway Code and book as many driving lessons as you think you will need. If you can get parents or friends to give you regular driving practice, so much the better. Then have confidence in yourself! If you know what you are doing and have had enough driving experience, you should view the driving test as just that, a test to put you on the road, rather than some awful mountain you will never climb.

## Try it now

* Sit down and relax.
* Take three deep breaths in through the nose and out through the mouth.
* Visualize yourself feeling calm and stress-free.
* Picture yourself driving confidently and competently.
* See in your mind's eye the examiner giving you a pass.

Walk up to the examiner with a smile. Look upon him as someone who is there to help you to pass the test. When you get into the car, take a moment to relax and get yourself comfortable, adjusting the seat if necessary. Breath deeply, as this will help to lower your heart rate, and tell yourself that you will stay calm. Don't rush, as this can lead to panic. Keep breathing slowly and steadily, and visualize success.

**Remember this**

The more you are able to relax, the more you will feel able to cope.

This will increase your confidence.

## Making a complaint

BLAST! No, I am not swearing; B.L.A.S.T. is something that people working in customer services will be aware of as part of their training. To know how customer service staff are trained will help when making a complaint.

▶ B is for Believing you have a grievance.

▶ L is for Listening to your complaint.

▶ A is for Acting on what you have told them.

▶ S is for Service to make sure things are put right in the future.

▶ T is for Thank you for telling them what went wrong.

All companies should look at complaints as feedback, because if customers don't complain about a product or service that is not up to scratch, how will the company ever know? But it is the way the complaint is made that is significant. Your body language is crucial if you are to get the best results.

▶ Try to avoid making a scene.

▶ Call the waiter or assistant to one side.

▶ Tell them quietly and calmly what is wrong.

▶ Keep your voice light.

▶ Stand or sit up straight.

▶ Look them in the eye.

▶ Smile!

It is easy to lose your temper if you and your guests have waited hours for a meal and when it arrives it is cold, or the dry cleaners have shrunk your favourite outfit. But if you raise your voice, your adversary (and the situation can become adversarial) will raise their voice, and the situation can soon become a slanging match.

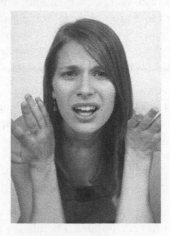

It is important to say when you are not pleased with the way you have been treated, but you will get much further if you are courteous. If a waitress asks 'Is everything all right?' and it patently isn't, tell her so.

▶ 'I am sorry, but the vegetables are cold. Could we have some fresh ones, please?'

▶ 'We ordered coffee a while ago now, is it on its way?'

▶ 'I am afraid this is my favourite dress and it has shrunk. What compensation can I expect?'

The main thing is to be clear about what you expect, and firm about what you will accept. Be polite and you will find disputes are settled quicker and more pleasantly. A complaint made in this way will not antagonize and will allow you to keep control of the situation, because you appear reasonable, and get the best results or compensation.

## Try it now

✻ Using your mobile phone, practise making a complaint.
✻ Record your voice, then play back the recording and analyse it.

# Dealing with the bereaved

Bereavement is a distressing experience not only for the bereaved but for those around them. Some people find it very awkward to know what to say to a grieving friend or relative. Having lost my brother and my partner unexpectedly within six weeks of each other, I have had first-hand experience of this.

Everyone who loses a loved one wants to talk about that person; it is a way of keeping them alive – people live on in the memories of others – so my advice is to say what you feel and tell them how sorry you are. But be aware of their body language. If somebody who has suffered a loss turns their head away or you see tears in their eyes when you start to relive memories, it is time to change the subject gently.

About six months after a bereavement, much of the attention and comfort that has surrounded a family starts to peter out, and that is the time when many people need support. Watch out for a faraway look, or the unconscious wringing of hands or fiddling with rings at a social occasion; these are signs that all is not well. I have found that cheerful conversation about the departed will often provide comfort as it helps to share memories. On the other hand, it is also important for those who are grieving to try to be positive. We are all sympathetic towards someone for a time, but after a while someone who is drooping with misery will drive people away because, human nature being what it is, we all feel uncomfortable with someone who is constantly depressed and despondent.

Funerals can be either solemn occasions or joyous affairs, and clergy have to learn to read the body language of bereaved families in order to assess their needs and counsel them sympathetically. Dealing with a death may be an almost everyday event for the clergy, but for the relatives it is a stressful and deeply upsetting time and they need to feel that they are talking to someone compassionate and sensitive. Active listening is crucial, as is constant eye contact, in encouraging people in distress to open up and say what is really on their minds. But putting on a happy face really does help lift your feelings, and looking to the future rather than harking back to the past is vital in forging a new life after a death.

## Answers to the self-assessment

1 Through positive posture
2 They help to slow your heart rate
3 To be polite
4 To be prepared
5 Because they are the first things people will assess you on
6 Breathe deeply
7 At the trial of O. J. Simpson
8 'Thank you'
9 Because they provide feedback
10 By agitated body language, such as hand-wringing, a faraway look or tears in the eyes, constant swallowing, lip-licking.

## Focus points

The main points to remember from this chapter are:
* be aware of your image
* be prepared mentally
* visualize a successful outcome
* be polite when making complaints
* be positive.

# Index